~ue

Memories of a Cape Breton Childhood

971
.69
503
092
Peach

Peach, Earle.
   Memories of a Cape Breton childhood / Earle Peach.
-- Halifax, N.S. : Nimbus, c1990.
   130 p. : ill.

04214757   ISBN:0921054416 (pbk.)

1. Peach, Earle. 2. Black Brook (N.S.) - Biography. 3.
Cape Breton Island (N.S.) - Biography. I. Title

Memories
of a
Cape Breton
Childhood

Earle Peach

NIMBUS PUBLISHING LIMITED

Nimbus Publishing Limited
P.O. Box 9301, Station A
Halifax, Nova Scotia
B3K 5N5

Design: Arthur Carter, Halifax
Photographs: Earle Peach, Public Archives of Nova Scotia, Miners
    Museum
Back-Cover Photograph: Van's Studio, Ottawa

Canadian Cataloguing in Publication Data

Peach, Earle.

Memories of a Cape Breton Childhood

ISBN 0-921054-41-6

1. Peach, Earle. 2. Black Brook (N.S.)—Biography.
3. Cape Breton Island (N.S.)—Biography. I. Title.

FC2349.B52Z49 1990 971.6'9503'092 C90-097538-5
F1039.5.B52P42 1990

Printed and bound in Canada

In fond memory of my parents

Contents

L'Envoi

Into my heart an air that kills
From yon far country blows:
What are those blue remembered hills,
What spires, what farms are those?

That is the land of lost content,
I see it shining plain,
The happy highways where I went
And cannot come again.

—A.E. Housman

Prologue

Although we arrived on the scene in the same year and within four days of each other, I am inclined to doubt that Halley's comet had chosen to mark this occasion. Without all the calendar juggling by popes and emperors, however, the two events could have coincided exactly. Adolf Hitler had also chosen April 20 for his début, and his later undoing seems to indicate that he was not quite in phase with the comet, as I was. The law of averages suggests that millions of other people must have arrived on the planet on April 20, 1910, in more or less favourable climes, most of whom have taken off by now for latitudes unknown while only a handful of them hang around to write memoirs.

The comet, of course, was not exactly a newcomer, for the Greeks had noted it a few hundred years B.C., and it reappeared recently. I am fairly confident that in spite of eerily fantastic dreams at times, this is my first time around, and I am untroubled by visions of having been a prophet of Ancient Israel, a Persian-rug vendor of Omar Khayyám's time, or a conspirator in the Gunpowder Plot, all of which leaves me with a blank page—a thing I detest!

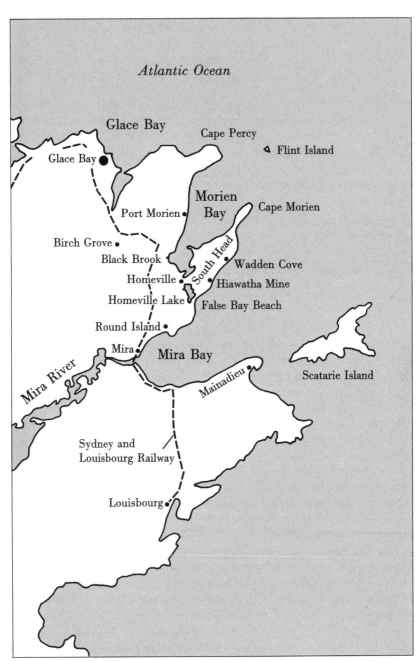

Atlantic Ocean

Glace Bay

Cape Percy

◁ Flint Island

Glace Bay ●

Morien
Bay

Cape Morien

Port Morien ●

Birch Grove ●

Black Brook

Wadden Cove ●

Homeville ●

Hiawatha Mine ●

South Head

Homeville Lake

False Bay Beach

Round Island ●

Mira ●

Mira Bay

Mira River

Mainadieu ●

Scatarie Island

Sydney and
Louisbourg Railway

Louisbourg ●

Southeastern Cape Breton

Home and Family

Chapter One

My earliest conscious memory is of being picked up out of bed by Father and carried downstairs to the kitchen, where we remained for some time looking out the north window toward the brook and the smoking slate dump a mile away. As he held me, I was told that overnight I had acquired by some means a new sister and that this creature was now in the parlour with Mother. I felt that something momentous had occurred, for it was not his custom to carry me downstairs, and besides, he was home from work and it did not seem to be Sunday.

My next memory is of running across the field closely pursued by my brother and going back into the house feeling a knifelike pain in my chest which made it hard to breathe. Then I have vague memories of the doctor and of a lot of talk and of ages and ages in bed during which time I had to urinate in an old green bottle. I had pneumonia, and the chances of recovery at the time were about fifty-fifty. The scars of this attack were to plague me at various times in later life. I may have been months recovering from it, and the incident must have followed closely upon the birth of my sister Evelyn. When finally able to sit up and look out the window, I saw a white pig hanging on a tripod by the barn, the annual sacrificial victim. Evelyn had arrived in August; the pig was always killed in October. It was 1913.

My home turned out to be a tiny boxlike structure set on flat stones and partially hollowed out underneath for a root cellar reached by lifting up a hatch in the floor of the living room. In winter it was banked up heavily around the sides with eel grass gathered on the shores a mile away and hauled home by boat. It had no storm windows, so in winter the panes were always heavily coated with frost so that you could draw on them and make pictures. Heat was supplied by a coal fireplace in the living room and an Enterprise range in the kitchen. "Duff," or coal, was cheap or free. On Sunday evening a fire was lit in the heater in the parlour for the hymn session and later in a similar stove in the upstairs hall.

Four tiny bedrooms upstairs had been completed one by one as the family expanded, but when the number reached six, all space, even with doubling up, had been pre-empted. A ladder on the wall in the boys' room led to a miniature attic above the eaves to reveal that the builder, John Martell, had widely miscalculated the position of the chimney with respect to the roof opening in the peak, causing the former to lean at an angle of eighty-five degrees; it was sustained in that position by a heavy timber. I have heard since that John had a patent on this type of chimney building.

Everyday access to the house was through a small porch attached to the kitchen; the "front" door, facing the highway, was reserved for special occasions or people, as was the parlour, whose drawn curtains, gloom, and air of mustiness gave it the proper atmosphere for singing hymns, entertaining rare visitors, and serving as a "lying-in" room for Mother. A narrow pantry across the end of the kitchen held the cooking utensils, a barrel of flour, a smaller barrel of sugar, shelves for cookie tins and spices, the churn and, of course, the big weekly jar of buttermilk. All meals except Sunday dinner were eaten in the kitchen, where a pipe from the stove passed through the ceiling to a small chimney above. This was a natural fire trap which waited patiently for thirty-five years for its moment of triumph, when Sister, having stoked up a hot fire to bake a cake, left the house to visit a neighbour.

A narrow lane separated the house from a garden surrounded by a high picket fence. Cultivation was intense in this garden, for it contained six apple trees, a dozen currant and gooseberry bushes, and beds of perennial flowers, with space left over for carrots, onions, beets, rhubarb, tomatoes, and lettuce, all in an area of thirty-five by fifty feet. The remainder of the one-acre lot (excluding a small cow pasture too wet and rocky to cultivate), extending along the side of the brook, included potatoes, hay, and oats for the cow.

It was miserable clay soil from which Father annually extracted dozens and dozens of wheelbarrow loads of rocks, which he dumped over the bank, an unending work project that provided valuable disciplinary labour for his sons, ensuring that their hands were not left at the disposal of Satan. The ancient glacier had distributed its load indiscriminately and impartially, and I am confident that this acre could provide employment for many additional generations of rock pickers without even slightly exhausting its generous supply.

Adjacent to the kitchen stood the "duff house," in which was stored this coal product, gathered in bags along the shores and brought home by rowboat. A few feet to the south was the "storehouse," later to be converted into a garage which held the staple supply of salt herring, mackerel, cod, and pork and in winter the annual "quarter" of beef. Here too on a small workbench reposed Father's sacred tool chest, containing

The Peach home was a small boxlike structure in Black Brook, Cape Breton.

a handsaw or two, a few chisels, hammers, and planes. Dire penalties threatened those rash enough to tamper with its contents, and when one did, much care was taken to replace them in the usual order and thus avoid the menacing "Who's been in my tool chest?"

Next to this was the barn, which housed not only the cow and her food supply but also sloped down on one side to cover the henhouse, where thirty-five or forty hens toiled to help pay the grocery bill. Only on special occasions did one get an egg to eat. Because the hens had full access to the manure pile, their production, in colour and flavour, had a distinctly epicurean quality totally absent in the pallid, lack-lustre items now purchased in cardboard cartons.

Near this, in his house and outdoor pen, dwelt the annual pig, whose ritual sacrifice beclouded early childhood days. Here each cute little porker romped and frisked, grunted, squealed, rooted, and snuffed his way to 250 or 300 pounds, fed on odds and ends from the kitchen and a few bags of meal. By late fall he had grown to be one of us, part of the family. But the day of reckoning was at hand. One bright morning the side of his pen was unceremoniously broken down, and before he could protest this unusual action, he was bashed over the head with an axe, inverted while still squealing, and treacherously stabbed between the front legs with a long, keen knife.

After staggering around for a minute or two with great gouts of blood gushing from his wound, he expired with a groan and rolled over. A tackle was then attached to his legs to suspend him on a tripod, from which he was lowered into a puncheon of boiling water. He was not only dead but desecrated, our poor, poor pig. No one had begged his pardon or explained to him the necessity of this dire cruelty. Indian hunters were much more polite than this!

Human memories, fortunately, are short, and by the time he had passed through the boiling water, been suspended on the tripod to dry, and a few days later dismembered and carved, the shock of his demise had been largely forgotten. By winter, when his home-cured hams graced a dull bill of fare, the last of the animists had been reconverted.

As far as I know, no wedding pictures exist of my parents Sanford and Addie, but I assume they were married in the Baptist church at Homeville, Cape Breton, some time in 1902 by the Reverend Earle Kinley, a revivalist who visited there for a year or two. Brother Harold's second name was Kinley, while I inherited the Earle. Sister Nettie, with Martell as a second name, marked the predominant ancestry of that name, for both grandmothers were Martells.

A small studio photo taken in 1904 included the first born. Father was then thirty, Mother, twenty-eight, and their facial expressions show that male authority was to rule the roost. Mother, shy, meek, retiring; Father, head tilted upward, one hand hooked across his chest in his watch chain, son of Governor Tom, who had also ruled the roost. Neither is smiling, for having a photo taken was a serious business, and it cost money. Sister Nettie was also present and probably a good reason for the inordinate pride on Father's part; he had sired a child.

At the time of their marriage Father was employed firing a boiler at the old coal-washing plant a mile distant, which had polluted Black Brook, the tidal stream that we lived beside. After leaving school at the end of Grade Four, he had toiled for his father as a fisherman until age twenty-one, and previous to his job at the wash plant he had worked for some time in Sydney building a pier. I was to hear many times of the evil paths he had fallen into in this period, when every Saturday night he visited a saloon and had a beer. Then righteousness fell upon him, and turning his face to the wall, he abjured alcohol for all time, except as manifested in spruce beer or home-brew made from blueberries. I can recall one occasion when, having entrusted this concoction to mature in a galvanized pail, he found it had brightened its inside considerably. But, being a resolute man, he quaffed a hearty drink of the beverage and was ill for several hours—not drunk, just poisoned.

By the time I was born, the wash plant had burned down and he had become a carpenter at No. 22 Colliery at Birch Grove, about two miles distant, a position he held until its closing in the 1930s. Three huge books on steam engineering in our homemade bookcase must have been a relic of failed ambitions following the demise of the wash plant. No one ever opened them. Despite his early departure from school, Father became an avid reader, the only one in his family to do so. By 1914 we were getting the *Sydney Post*, the *Orange Sentinel*, the *Family Herald*,

Addie and Sanford Peach were "quite devoted" to each other.

the *Christian Herald* (a British publication), and the *Maritime Baptist* (Grandmother's delight). In the early days his habit of reading aloud to the family various serialized stories in the *Christian Herald* no doubt quickened our interest in private reading. Bible readings and family prayers were also featured.

Throughout her life Mother was the workhorse and worrier of the family, and her relations with my father Sanford were not improved by having her mother Adelaide in permanent residence up to her death in 1925. As the ruling force in her own household, because of a rather ineffectual husband, she found it difficult to accept her daughter's quick surrender to male authority, and as a Martell whose family descent unquestionably outranked that of the "Johnny-come-lately" Peaches, she no doubt found it difficult to submit to one; after all, her elder daughter Annie, who lived next door had lost no time in establishing matriarchal superiority over Uncle Tim and family.

What would have happened if Sanford had married Annie God alone knows. As things were, they could never agree on anything; Annie was a fanatic Liberal who read the *Montreal Witness* and Father a flat-out Tory. Uncle Tim, who could barely read, stuck to knitting headings for his lobster traps. On Sunday mornings, though, in a loud word-by-word monotone, he read the weekly Sunday-school lesson to his children.

What I have said in no way implies a strife-ridden atmosphere at home, for Mother and Father were quite devoted to each other. Before marriage neither had had any companion of the opposite sex, hence what little they knew about sex they had learned from each other. I do remember Father telling us once that at one time he had had a crush on a distant cousin from Mira Gut but had soon found that a seven-mile walk was a bit too much for a working man.

In their bedroom, as each of the family was to discover privately, reposed the "holy of holies," Father's trunk. Inside it, in a blue-covered volume entitled *The Light of Life*, written by a Victorian clergyman, lay exposed all the secrets of sex and married life, including the grim warning that the practice of "the secret vice" never failed to lead to idiocy and damnation. Victims of such a practice were even illustrated for those who might doubt. As a man who even in his late years was reputed to be strongly sexually inclined, Father had probably read this volume too late and had been rescued only by marriage. His sons (and perhaps his daughters) were not so lucky and over the years staggered under the guilt of a forfeited Eden. Worry, worry, worry!

It was not the custom then for parents to bestow gushing affection on their children or to receive it in return, for the very good reason that they were too busy to do so, and that families were usually much larger. You fed and clothed them, taught them to obey, and called the doctor if they became seriously ill.

The Black Brook Peaches were Baptists, unlike their Anglican cousins in Port Morien, and as I found only in late years, this was due to the Martell matriarchy. How some of the Martells had deviated from the Anglican faith will be detailed later. Suffice it to say at this point that neither of my grandfathers had had any serious religious commitment and left such trifling matters to their wives, who handled them most effectively. We grew up with the firm conviction that by abstaining from the Demon Rum, the Devil's playing cards, and any plan or unnecessary work on the Sabbath, we would be assured of a higher status in heaven than those who tolerated such evils. Although this negative attitude gave us a fine glow of superiority, I cannot feel that it was balanced by many positive factors, for the Peach brothers were no more kind or loving toward each other, or toward their families or wives, than the occasion demanded, and none was particularly charitable.

One of the early Martells had become an outstanding Baptist minister who preached across Nova Scotia, and this was never forgotten. After learning the alphabet from the letters on the old Enterprise range in the kitchen, I soon mastered the art of reading so effectively that I had covered the Grade One reader before entering school and was placed in Grade Two. For lack of other books, I sometimes gathered together three or four bibles to see if the texts were the same. Grandmother and my parents saw in this phenomenon a sure indication that in my future career I would emulate the great work of my illustrious distant relative, and they lost no time in making this hope known to their friends. Thus at an early age I had directed myself toward university by unwittingly raising in my parents' minds an illusive hope. I did reach university, but the spark from heaven was never to be kindled.

Pioneers

Chapter Two

In recent years the study of genealogy seems to have reached new peaks, as those who by some means have attained wealth or public attention seek to attribute that success to their descent from some illustrious ancestor. Following such devious paths, one eliminates all the undesirable and unmentionable factors and ends up as a direct descendant of Julius Caesar, William the Conqueror, or Henry VIII. If I were seriously disposed in this direction, I would no doubt have to insist upon my descent from that glorious Charles Martell, the grandson of Charlemagne who triumphed over the Moors in 729 A.D. Any tendency in this direction, however, is cooled off somewhat by sport spoilers such as Professor J.H. Plumb, the well-known English historian: "After the lapse of a mere twenty generations, everyone has 1,048,576 direct ancestors ... great, great, great, etc., grandparents. Apart from a few immigrant groups, every Englishman of English grandparents may claim to be descended from everyone who was alive in England at the Norman Conquest ... so much for Norman descent."

In light of this discouraging pronouncement, and considering that the Battle of Tours preceded the Norman Conquest by well over three hundred years, I could probably claim as close a relationship to the commander of the Moorish forces as to Charles Martell, despite old family traditions. Consequently, I shall limit my genealogical pursuits to no earlier date than the time of the arrival of my ancestors in Cape Breton, adding to that what little is known of their previous history and their reasons for emigration.

The first on the scene, and undoubtedly one of the first settlers in Cape Breton, was Charles Martell (1733-1819). This Charles is no legendary figure, for his activities, particularly in the religious field, are catalogued in the annals of St. George's Anglican Church in Sydney, and the mortal remains of him and his wife repose under well-marked stones in the small, wind-swept Anglican cemetery at Mainadieu. Martell family histories have proliferated in the last hundred years, and their unanimity lends credence to the belief that their fortunes had declined from a much greater state.

According to their story, the Martells had been Huguenot noblemen. Following the Revocation of the Edict of Nantes in 1685, which had guaranteed their rights, a series of religious persecutions occurred, and in the following years 200,000 Huguenots were driven from France. The Martells had prospered in the linen industry around the Lyon area, and in a period of revival of persecution, Anthony Martell fled with his young wife and son, Charles, to Ireland. His mother, who insisted upon staying, fell victim to the purge.

In Ireland, the former count Anthony was soon to resume his interest in the linen industry and to prosper. A daughter was born to them. They must have remained there for some time, later at least than 1745, for when father and son emigrated to Halifax, Charles was old enough to take part in his father's business. Why they left Ireland is unknown, as is the fate of Anthony's wife and daughter. In setting up his Halifax venture, Anthony took on a partner. A few years later, while father and son were on a business trip to New York, Anthony contracted yellow fever and died. On his return to Halifax, Charles made the sad discovery that the partner had sold out their interests and decamped with the funds.

Not long after this, 1758, Wolfe arrived to organize his expedition against Louisbourg. Presumably because of his experience in business, Charles had little trouble in gaining the rank of sergeant in the Commissary Department. As far as is known, he left no memoirs of this experience, but he remained there after the fortress had fallen. Since Thomas, his first son, was born there in 1760, we can assume that he met and married his bride Anne Schmidt, a Waldensian refugee from Switzerland, while on furlough to Halifax in 1759.

Although he did not proceed with the expedition against Quebec, this year was a busy one, for Louisbourg was being used as a preparatory base for that undertaking. By the following year William Pitt, the British Prime Minister, fearing that some misguided diplomacy might return the island to the French, pronounced the sentence of death upon the fortress. In a letter dated February 9, sent to Amherst, he instructed him to "take the most timely and effectual care that all the fortifications of the Town of Louisbourg, together with all the works, and Defences whatever, belonging either to the said place, or to the Port, and Harbour, thereof, be forthwith totally demolished, and razed, and all materials so thoroughly destroyed, as that no use may, hereafter, be ever made of the same."

Anyone familiar with the site previous to 1950 will concede that the demolition squad did a thorough and painstaking job; the visitor today, however, will note that the last part of his order failed to be entirely executed. One can imagine that the young Martells grew up in a rather explosive atmosphere, for the first six of Charles's and Anne's family were born there, which brings us up to at least 1776. Some time later, land grants were assigned to deserving applicants who wished to remain in Cape Breton, but the first official confirmation of grants to Charles does not appear until 1791, at which time he received a grant of 130 acres at "Menadoo" and a further grant of 200 acres at Mira River.

The Mainadieu site was probably familiar to all those who had remained at Louisbourg, and Charles was no doubt only one among many who settled there. Sheltered, to a considerable extent by the island of Scatarie, from the worst ravages of the Atlantic, the little seaport of Mainadieu rapidly developed into a flourishing centre of trade with the Caribbean and the New England States, outdating Sydney as the island's chief port. One can speculate that before long, Charles was back in the drapery business there. For the younger generation, however, the lure of the sea proved too strong, and many Captain Martells lie buried in the later Mainadieu cemetery, while others lost their lives at sea.

By the time his beloved Anne had died in 1804, Charles had definitely become a member of the Establishment. Anglican-church records honour him with the title "Charles Martell, Esquire," and in the dearth of visiting clergy, he was granted the privilege of performing the rites of christening, marriage, and burial in his area. Many of his own children and grandchildren received some of these ceremonies from his hand.

As far as is known, two of his sons, Thomas and John, did not marry; John (1767-1836), who later had a grant of his own at Mainadieu, lies alone in the larger cemetery; the burial place of Thomas (who also had a grant) is unknown. Of four daughters—Jane, born in 1770, Anne, in 1772, Mary, in 1780—nothing is known, but Elizabeth, born between 1775, and 1779, married Joseph Dillon of Dublin, Ireland, a union that established the dynasty of Cape Breton Dillons.

Credit for the vast proliferation of Martells in the nineteenth and twentieth centuries thus falls upon the three remaining sons: Charles, born in 1763, Joseph, in 1775, and Anthony, in 1782. With fitting genealogical delight, I number two of these, Charles and Anthony, among my ancestors. By the time they had reached a marriageable age, the Loyalist immigrants had arrived on the scene to provide them with wives. Charles, who chose from them Susannah Mehitable Wilcox, fathered a family of nine, including two sea captains. His son Charles, born in 1793, married another Loyalist woman, Esther Spencer, daughter of Hezekiah. One of their six children, little Susannah Mehitable, was later to marry Thomas Martell, the sixth son of Anthony. Thus derive two of my great-grandparents, giving me my first surplus

SOUTH HEAD, MORIEN, C.B.

John Spencer, who married Stetson Holmes's daughter Clorinda, settled at South Head, overlooking Morien Bay.

of Martell genes. Anthony himself had married Lucinda Holmes, and of the Holmeses, much more anon.

Charles, the father of the sea captains, continued to live at Mainadieu for some time, as did Anthony. But Joseph, who married Patience Phipps, another Loyalist, soon moved to the Mira River grant, where four of their family of ten, were to marry Spencers. This is hardly surprising, as Joseph's three-hundred-acre grant adjoined the large Spencer grant, bordering the north side of the river at the Gut.

The exceptional hardships encountered by these early Cape Breton pioneers were due not only to the isolation of the Island itself, Halifax being the nearest settlement, a mere three hundred miles away, but also to the fact that each little community was isolated from the others by a complete lack of roads. Even much later than 1800, if we except a few muddy paths leading from Sydney into the environs, the only recognizable road was one constructed by the French. This connected Louisbourg to the upper Mira River area, where they had carried on some farming and lumbering activities to supply the garrison. Those first on the scene were much too busy trying to stay alive to worry about roads, and even to hack out footpaths through the jungles of spruce and alders in eastern Cape Breton must have been a formidable task. For the first forty or fifty years, therefore, all communication was by sea. One of the earliest recognizable roads led from Cow Bay (Port Morien) to Sydney, bypassing Glace Bay for the very good reason that there was no settlement there. Over this road, Grandmother Murrant used to say, food supplies were often carried on foot from Sydney in times of need, which meant in months when the whole coast was blocked with ice drifts. This had happened within her memory, and she was born in 1837.

In 1800, Sydney consisted of a few scattered rows of hovels strung out on the little peninsula between the harbour and Muggah's Creek, and a few barracks housing the military establishment. As an independent entity for a while, the island had a governor of its own, and the activities of this self-rule could form the background for a good musical comedy. Letters, written by early British visitors to the scene, express only loathing and contempt for this extreme outpost and its inhabitants. Life at the time can best be reconstructed from an imaginative study of the archives of St. George's Anglican Church, whose clergy in flowing or cramped script, and in varied styles of laconic understatement, faithfully transcribed their triumphs and tragedies: "I then baptized privately the daughter of Major MacMartin and Mrs. Elijah Forrester ... I then buried the infant son of a mulatto woman...." In this remarkable record the crimes and follies of early Sydney are made manifest.

When Loyalist Stetson Holmes arrived on the scene, around 1795, he was not assigned to the Sydney area. Indeed his one-thousand-acre grant lay at least twenty miles from it in the midst of a wilderness of spruce trees. Here, on an elevated knoll of land overlooking the little river that connects Homeville Lake with the headwaters of Morien Bay, he and his family hastened to construct a log house and settle down to a new life, a life vastly different from the prosperous one he had known in Rutland, Vermont.

To a young man a drastic change of this nature would have presented nothing more than a challenge against the impossible, but Stetson was no longer young. Born in Pembroke, Massachusetts, he had married into the well-known Shurtleff family, prospered, established a comfortable home in Rutland, and raised a large family. In the aftermath of the Revolutionary War, the elder members of his family were apparently able to overcome the vindictive prejudices of the victors, or perhaps it had been a family of divided loyalties. At any rate, packing up his wife and the four youngest children, Clorinda, Viza, Lucinda, and Arnold, he set his face grimly against the past and headed into the unknown.

In the face of appalling hardships, he was to establish a new community, Homeville. Through an intricate pattern of intermarriage with other pioneer families, Homeville became a community that was to last in spirit for 120 years, the community in which I was to grow up, a community that has now vanished.

Driven, like the Greeks of old, to the sea, he soon discovered that his nearest port of supply was at Mainadieu, seven or eight miles across Mira Bay, the home of the Martells. In the course of time, random encounters soon led to a romance between Stetson's eldest daughter, Lucinda, and Anthony, the youngest son of Charles Martell, Esquire. In 1803, at the ages of seventeen and twenty-one, respectively, they were united in holy matrimony within the Anglican Communion in Sydney. Theirs was to prove a most fruitful marriage. Numbered among the six sons and five daughters, who lived to mature age and married, were two of my great-grandfathers: Arnold (1815-1884), who married Jane Lisby Huntington, and Thomas (1823-1894), who married his aforementioned first cousin Susan Mehitable Martell, daughter of Charles (III) and the unfortunate Esther Spencer, who died in her twenties after bearing six children.

But this was only the beginning of Stetson's contribution to the local gene pool. In the same year, daughter Clorinda married John Spencer, who had moved from Mira River and settled on a grant across from Stetson's on the opposite side of the river estuary, thus becoming a resident of South Head. In 1806 daughter Viza married Joel Noel Shepard, another incoming Loyalist, and settled on a grant eastward and adjacent to the Spencer claim. In 1816 son Arnold married Ann Martell, daughter of Joseph at Mira. In the wake of these four marriages Stetson Holmes became the proud grandfather of fifty-two children. Many of these, of course, did not survive to maturity, but when in 1824 at the age of seventy-one he was carried to the top of the little hill on his own property, overlooking the quiet cove at the upper reaches of Morien Bay, it must have been evident to all that a mighty patriarch had fallen in Israel.

How troubled in spirit the survivors of that day would have been could they have foreseen the callous desecration that would be wrought upon the site 125 years later, when gigantic shovels ground into it, overthrowing the crude head stones and scattering his bones, along with those of others, on Cape Breton highways! But by that time the Holmeses of Homeville were no more, and the spruce forests that Stetson and his son and grandsons had so laboriously cleared had crowded back almost to their original state. Even if the few remaining residents of the area had been aware of what was happening, few, if any, would have known that they owed their existence to him.

The Years of the Grandparents

Chapter Three

What Grandfather Thomas Peach may have lacked in formal education seems to have been well compensated for by his native intelligence, and at the age of twenty-three, when he married Jane Levina Martell, it must have been plain to him that the ancestral location on South Head held little prospect for the future. A fisherman had to have easy access to the sea, but he did not need to expose himself to its unpredictable violence. His brother John had already settled in Port Morien, and it is likely that by this time a fairly well-travelled road existed around the bay. In its course, about three miles west of Port Morien, it had to cross Black Brook, a tidal stream about forty feet wide at the northwest corner of the bay. From its estuary a narrow channel ran through the sand flats, out between the bars, and into the bay. At high tide a fairly large fishing boat could make its way up to the head of the brook, and when the trees had been cleared off, it would be possible to do some farming. In this sheltered area Thomas succeeded in obtaining a one-hundred-acre grant and settled down with Jane to raise a family.

Previous to its hopeless pollution, this stream, running back four or five miles into a swampy wilderness, abounded in trout and possibly salmon. On its southern side, just above the wooden bridge which then existed, Thomas built his first house. Ten years previously his sister Elizabeth had married George Martell, a grandson of Anthony, and they presumably had been living at Round Island. With an eye for neighbours (and possibly cash), Tom sold George a part of his grant, to the west of the new house. To George's brother Jim, who had married Martha Spencer, a grand-daughter of John, he sold a considerable acreage, directly across the brook from his own home. Thus was founded, between 1870 and 1897, the settlement of Black Brook.

A quarter-mile upstream the Martell brothers (and probably Thomas) constructed a dam across the stream and, in a sluice around its north end, installed an under-shot water wheel which powered large millstones. How successful this grist mill proved to be is not known, but its construction must have involved monumental labour. Odds are, the whole apparatus was soon swept away in a spring freshet, leaving only the two massive stones and the huge iron shaft connecting them. One of these still remains on the spot in the woods; the other was at some time transported to Jim's house for a doorstep.

A mile upstream from this, George and Thomas secured grants enclosing part of the grassy meadows bordering the brook, from which shoulder-high grass could be mowed and harvested as winter fodder for their cows and horses. All three were still fishermen, and their efforts at agriculture were aimed solely at self-sustenance; it was not a market-gardening area. Still, a hard life of unremitting toil, compared with what Thomas had known on South Head, it must have seemed a Garden of Eden.

In time he was to prosper, to become known as a solid and respectable citizen, and a shrewd investor and lender of money. By the end of the century he and Jane had accumulated five sons and four daughters; George Martell, three sons and four daughters; James, three sons and five daughters. These were the associates, and this the community known to my father Sanford (Sandy) Peach, Tom's second son, born in 1876.

Needless to say, by this time the whole surrounding area had undergone a profound change since Stetson Holmes and John Spencer had established themselves amid the primeval forests. The period of mere survival had ended; strong sons, under their fathers' stern regimen, had not only expanded the paternal cleared acreage but had also hacked out of the wilderness establishments of their own, married neighbouring daughters, and raised large families. As noted previously, Cow Bay (Port Morien) had blossomed into a busy coal-mining and coal-shipping depot, houses had mushroomed along its northern side, and a thriving market had developed there, and in Glace Bay in the 1850s, for agricultural products as well as for the riches of the sea. This was to be the economy of my grandfathers, but unknown to the beneficiaries of this sudden prosperity, Cow Bay was experiencing its Golden Age, and by the turn of the century the decline had set in, which was to culminate in it becoming the insignificant residential area of the present.

On South Head my grandparents William Henry and Adelaide probably benefited from the upsurge at Cow Bay, but for some reason or other William failed to reach the state of affluence of Thomas at Black Brook. Between the years 1866 and 1890 they produced a family of one son and five daughters, the second youngest of whom became my mother, Adelaide, born in 1878. The son, Arnold, and a daughter, Mildred, died young and unmarried. The other three sisters married and became my favourite aunts.

On his death pioneer Stetson Holmes had left his one-thousand-acre grant to his son Arnold, who was shortly to leave the original site and establish himself and Lucinda Martell, daughter of Joseph, on the northern shore of Homeville Lake in a spot well suited to farming. By 1850 his eldest son, Joseph, was farming not only his grandfather's first holding but had also carved out for himself an excellent farm on the northern limit of the grant, while brother Arnold farmed an area south of this. By 1881 Joseph, in two marriages, had sired a total of fifteen children, including five sons, not one of whom was to marry and produce offspring; only three of the daughters were to marry. On his death the new home beside the highway, a mile south of Black Brook, was left, with its fertile acres, to his son Ronald and daughter Katherine, neither of whom was to marry.

A similar fate was to overtake the descendants of brother Arnold, who married Anthony Martell's daughter Lucinda; only one son, Henry, survived, who married Clarissa, a daughter of James at Black Brook, but apparently they had no children. Two daughters married but, as far as is known, produced no children, and here the family ended.

A third son, William Lawrence, who had lived with his father beside the lake, was to ensure the Holmeses' descent for at least one more generation. His marriage to Caroline Martell, Anthony's second youngest daughter, produced a family of six sons, five of whom married and lived to inherit the large area surrounding the lake and its vicinity. Two of the children, a boy and a girl, drowned in the lake in 1871. A surviving daughter, Helen, married Frank Shepard, a grandson of Joel Noel. In 1920 two of the sons, William and Thomas (known locally as Uncle Will and Uncle Tom), still farmed their acres beside the lake. A third brother had died, while two others, John and Marshall, had abandoned their holdings and moved to Glace Bay. Their descendants, if any, were minimal.

The third and fourth sons, Galen and Stetson, fared no better; of five sons born to the former, three died before age sixteen, and the remaining two did not marry. A similar fate befell Stetson's two sons. Thus when "Uncle Will" died in 1949 at the venerable age of ninety-four, the Holmes family had disappeared from Homeville, and few if any descendants of that name were living on Cape Breton Island. One hundred and sixty-two years had seen this family begin, bloom, and disappear, while the Martells, Spencers, Shepards, Peaches, and Murrants continued to populate the island and to spread over North America, even if few remained in the original area of settlement.

Cow Bay (c. 1867), known as Port Morien after 1895, blossomed into a busy coal-mining town during the latter half of the nineteenth century.

How had the descendants of John Spencer and Clorinda Holmes fared in the interim? Between the eldest son, George, born in 1804, and the youngest, Theophilus, lay a gap of twenty-four years and thirteen other children. By the time the latter married Ann Peters in 1857, George's eldest son, Hezekiah (Kyer), already had a son and two daughters and was shortly to acquire another four sons and two daughters. If land was to be assigned to George's other sons, Amos, Nathaniel, and Stephen, as well as to his brothers Arnold, Henry, and Theophilus, something had to give.

A mile to the northwest, across the headwaters of the bay, Henry and Theophilus secured a grant of 144 acres; immediately south of this, Nathaniel ended up with a 300-acre grant. Arnold received a grant of 100 acres a mile west of Port Morien; Hezekiah, Amos, and Stephen divided up the original grant on South Head. The Census of 1871 indicates that two of John's unmarried daughters were maintaining a household of their own, presumably in his first dwelling, until the first died in 1902 at the age of eighty-seven. In 1920 the Spencer property on South Head was owned or occupied by Willie, a son of Stephen, Albert, a son of Amos, and Howard, a son of Kyer. The only property remaining in the family at present is the grant assigned to Theophilus on the opposite side of the estuary, where Edith Spencer, his granddaughter (Mrs. Allison Ferguson), still maintains her household.

Meanwhile, the other Spencer families in Mira and the Martell families in Round Island, Mira, and Mainadieu had proliferated beyond belief. Many had left the area and established themselves in Sydney, in other parts of Nova Scotia, and in various parts of the United States and Canada. After three generations the tendency in the Martell family to cling to the hereditary names Charles, Anthony, John, Thomas, and Joseph, many of them contemporary with each other, would baffle any attempt at genealogy except that undertaken by computer.

By the 1970s economic changes had rendered the role of the small fishermen-farmer obsolete; the Murrants, Spencers, Shepards, and Peaches had disappeared from South Head, the Holmeses from Homeville; very few Spencers or Martells remained in Round Island or Mira, while in Mainadieu, the Martell ancestral home, one Martell family remained, whose breadwinner worked at the Sydney Steel plant. The irony of such changes can only be fully apparent to one who has undertaken a study of the area cemeteries; scores of Martells, many of them sea captains, are buried at Mainadieu, scores of Spencers in a private cemetery by Mira River, scores of Holmeses in the Baptist cemetery at Homeville.

In the long run, amusingly enough, the Peaches, who had survived the most hellish pioneer environment of all, were to prove the most adaptable to surviving in that particular area. Enough fifth-generation Peaches still live in Port Morien (descendants of John) to form a good-sized male choir, while in Black Brook Tom's grandson is raising a family of sons in the last house that Tom was to build.

We must keep in mind, that though all were pioneers, the Murrants and Peaches arrived at least one generation later than the Holmeses and the Spencers and two generations later than the Martells. If late arrival on the land had prejudiced the geographical location of the Murrants, their fortune was indeed blessed compared with the fate of the Peaches. By 1820 all arable land on the Morien side of the head had probably been claimed and settled, while on the Mira Bay side the Waddens, Boutiliers, and others had shrunk as far westward as they could. So to the east of these, in the most forbidding settled location on the head, Robert Peach and his family were to put down roots—if roots could grow amid such desolation.

In the genealogical tree, as in any other tree, the upper branches have received more sunlight and are thus more clearly defined than the lower ones. The Martells, Holmeses, and Spencers had inherited from previous generations a definite pride in their family backgrounds; they had known circumstances much more favourable than those into which they had moved and were confident that in time they would regain in the new land some of the status they had known in the old. Family history was important to them, for it acted as a guide toward their restoration. Histories of the Martells have abounded for the last century or so.

In contrast, it might be noted that Thomas Murrant carried his history with him, and except for oral tradition, it was to end with him. In the case of the Peaches, however, the task of the historian becomes even more difficult, for Robert Peach did not even bring a legend with him to pass on to succeeding generations. The story of the family must thus be reconstructed almost entirely from official records and such vague memories as "they used to say."

Although by no means a common name—I have been unable thus far to find it in books listing family names—it is definitely of English origin but seems more likely to have derived from the French *pêche* and *pêcheur* than from the attractive and luscious fruit. It is still well known around the Cornwall and Devon coasts of England. Peach emigrants were known to be among the early American colonists (one by that name was hanged for robbing and killing an Indian), and in the twentieth century Peach families have migrated to western Canada.

From the best information available, two Peach brothers, Andrew and Robert, left Somerset, England, shortly before 1800. Andrew settled in Newfoundland, where the family is still well known; Robert, who married Jane Andrews, settled in Sydney. Tradition has it that their departure had something to do with tea smuggling. Another tradition states that an early Peach once owned the land now occupied by the Sydney Steel plant. That this may contain an element of truth is shown by the address assigned to the family in the record of St. George's Anglican Church. A Louise Peach, daughter of Robert and Jane, was christened in 1814; the family address is Sydney Harbour.

It is possible that Robert was married at the time of his arrival, for the birth dates of the family as shown in the christening records are as follows: Martha, 1798, Robert, 1804, Jane, 1807, Susan, 1808, James, 1812, Nancy, 1813, Louise, 1814, Thomas, 1815. Civic records of the period show that Robert Peach served occasionally as foreman of the Jury, attending to the intense civil and criminal litigation common to pioneer years. Other than this, there is silence.

Another tradition, this time passed on by my father, is that an early Peach drank himself out of his Sydney property, and in view of the next family move, there is a certain inescapable logic in this belief. Nothing but a major disaster could have impelled the family into leaving the relatively pleasant confines of Sydney Harbour to settle on the bleakest, most barren southeast coast of South Head. Yet an early land-grant map shows that a grant of 141 acres was assigned to Robert Peach on this site. It can be assumed that he and his family were fishermen, and it is just possible that this was the only unclaimed fishing site in the coastal area near Sydney at the time they had to move. That this Robert Peach was dead by 1842 is certain, for Robert junior and Widow Peach were in that year presented as candidates for confirmation.

The three sons evidently continued to live for some time at the new location. Robert junior married Hannah Forbes in 1832, and about the same time, great-grandfather James married Margaret (last name unknown). Early in his career James had both legs frozen and had to have them removed about a foot below the knee; the rest of his life he spent walking on the stumps, protected only by some sort of leather shoes. Whether this catastrophe occurred before or after his marriage is unknown, for the marriage is unrecorded in the annals, though that of Robert and Hannah is, as are the christenings of James's family. A frequently repeated family tradition has it that there is Indian blood in the Peach family, and if true, this is its source. The unknown Margaret is sometimes claimed to have been an Indian or, alternately, as having been one of two white girls raised by an Indian woman. It seems unlikely that the mystery will ever be solved, for those who may have known the answer have long departed.

What I also find puzzling is the lack of detail regarding the loss of James's legs; that it happened is unquestionable, yet Father, who was sixteen years old when his grandfather died, and must have remembered him quite well, never discussed the grim trial that led to the amputations, if he himself knew it. The freezing was supposed to have occurred from exposure at sea, and there the matter ended. It may have been that the generation gap in the Peach family was wider than usual, or it may have been that in the formative years I evinced no more interest in the past than my eighteen-year-old son does today when he says, "Oh, now you're bringing that up again!" At any rate the story remains untold.

What can be confirmed from official records is that between 1833 and 1852, James and Margaret brought forth a brook of three sons and four daughters; gaps of three and four years in the records probably indicate others who died young. The Census of 1871 indicates the following disposition of the Peach families: James's elder brother Robert had died, and his widow, Hannah, was living with son William and his family of seven. Younger brother Thomas had married and settled in Big Lorraine, near Louisbourg, with a family of two sons. James's elder son, John, had married and was living in Port Morien with a family of two sons and a daughter. Grandfather Thomas was apparently living alone with a younger brother, James, while his father had remarried and produced another family of three sons, the eldest of whom had been born in 1860. By 1888 all three had died of tuberculosis, the scourge of so many early families.

Not far from the grave of great-grandfather Thomas Murrant, in the Anglican cemetery, lie a series of mounds marked by a single stone engraved with the name of James Peach (1812-1892) and the names of the three later sons, whom he survived. No trace indicates that either of his wives is buried there, this in contrast to the Spencers and Murrants on whose stones the names of husband and wife both appear. And in the little church a stained-glass window is dedicated to the memory of James Peach. The rest, as Shakespeare says, is silence.

Assuredly none of the second generation had undergone the tribulations of this Job-like character. Despite his enormous physical handicap he had lived a life of unremitting toil and raised two families, only to see the second, of whom he was extremely fond, drop off one by one in his old age. What sort of man was he? It seems extremely unlikely that anyone living in 1970 could have known him, yet such, oddly enough, happens to be the truth.

While visiting Sydney in that year, I met in the Cove (a very pleasant senior citizens' home) Mrs. Beatrice MacDonald, a lady of ninety-three years, whose father, a Boutilier, was a son of Nancy Peach, a sister to James Peach. She could remember that when she was a small girl the old man used to come to visit them in Sydney. He seemed very fond of her, and she thought of him as a wonderful person, very kind, who always brought her a present.

I can recall that in my youth a small "tin-type" photograph of him still hung on the wall in my uncle's living room, and I was told that this was my great-grandfather. It was a pleasant but very determined face, ringed around with a fringe of beard. The eyes looked defiantly forward, and even a child could sense the authority they proclaimed. His word was not to be trifled with, and this attitude he was to bequeath to his descendants.

The Baptist Revival

Chapter Four

By 1824 my great-grandfathers were of the following ages: Thomas Murrant, Jr., 11, James Peach, 12, Arnold Martell, 9, and Thomas Martell, 1; by 1851 the last of the grandparents, Jane Levina Martell, had been born. Up until the latter date nothing significant had occurred to change the style of living from that of the previous generation. True, families had expanded, farms had expanded, fishing boats had multiplied, and corduroy roads, through the bush and swamps, connected the settlements. The enormous influx of Scottish immigrants into the area, beginning in 1840, soon left little land unassigned, though few of them reached South Head or Homeville. Because the majority of these were Roman Catholics, intermarriages between them and the families whose fortunes we are pursuing were rare; these were to continue intermarrying with each other, even to a first-cousin degree of relationship, and I can find no trace of Scottish ancestry in my descent, which for a Cape Bretoner, is unusual.

Another restricting influence on the choice of eligible marriage partners occurred in the 1840s when the families were rent asunder by the Baptist religious revival. For this story we must return to the annals of the Mainadieu Martells.

As noted previously, Stetson Holmes's daughter Lucinda had married Anthony Martell, youngest son of Charles, Esquire, and for some years the family had continued to live there. Licences of occupation of Mainadieu had been granted by the government of Nova Scotia as early as 1768, long antedating the arrival there of Charles Martell. Population figures of 1788 show 107 living there, against 51 in Louisbourg, 5 in Cow Bay, and 209 in Sydney. As the latter would have included a military establishment, the civilian population of Mainadieu was considerably in excess of that of Sydney. As fishing lots and log houses expanded, a generation of sea captains were soon carrying on a brisk trade with the West Indies, South America, Spain, the Mediterranean, and the New

England States, the chief export being dried salt cod; the chief imports, molasses, sugar, and rum, the chosen beverage of all true Cape Bretoners.

Shortly before 1818 it had become plain to Lucinda, if not to Anthony, that the raucous and rowdy atmosphere of Mainadieu was hardly a fitting environment in which to rear Stetson Holmes's grandchildren (five sons and three daughters). We can imagine that there was much searching of heart between the two concerning this matter, but finally, if we can credit the story told in a 1906 issue of the *Maritime Baptist*, the family decided to leave the land of "strong drink" and migrate to Round Island, on the opposite side of Mira Bay. This decision, which brought the family into closer contact with the Holmeses and the Spencers, was to have far-reaching effects on the days of my youth. To quote the *Maritime Baptist*:

> From the time they settled at Round Island until 1837, the Rev. Mr. Inglis [Bishop Inglis] visited the place once a year to preach in private homes and sprinkle all the new babies in the community. In the year 1837 Rev. Maynard Parker visited the place and presented Jesus Christ as the only Saviour for lost men apart from any church-connection or church ordinances. The following year the Rev. David McQuillan proclaimed the same message of salvation from one end of the community to the other, and a deep conviction of sin took hold of the consciences of young and old.

In historical perspective, what had occurred at Mira was a long-overdue shock wave from the western end of the province, where fifty years before, Henry Alline, an uneducated and untrained self-appointed revivalist, had successfully challenged the reigning religious establishments. In his nine-year campaign he had shown that the "inner light," rather than years of theological training, was the real criterion of a messenger of God.

To continue the quotation from the article, written by a later Martell:

> Samuel Spencer [son of Hezekiah] who had married Anthony Martell's eldest daughter [actually his third daughter, Sophia] was the first to accept Jesus Christ as a personal Saviour and he rejoiced greatly in the light. His vision of God was so clear and abiding that he went from house to house calling upon the people to repent of sin and lay hold of eternal life through Jesus Christ.
>
> The following year George Armstrong, then a young man studying at Horton Academy [Wolfville], returned to his home in Sydney, heard of the great work of grace at Mira, visited the place, and rejoiced greatly at the presence and power of God in saving people. He sent for Rev. Joseph

Dimock, who came and baptized large numbers of people in the name of the Lord Jesus and organized them into a Baptist church.

On one beautiful Sunday morning, Arnold Martell, his wife Lucinda, and ten of their children were baptized, and the next Sunday the other two sons followed in the sacred ordinance ... a believing household.

This astounding reformation was to engulf not only Anthony Martell's family but also the large families of Hezekiah and Nathaniel Spencer, that of Arnold Holmes at Homeville, the Shepard and Peters families at South Head, and brother Joseph's family at Mira. The seafaring Martells at Mainadieu, however, seem to have continued in the paths of darkness, as did John Spencer and his family at South Head, who by this time was so far committed to the Established Church as to make any back-tracking impracticable. An irreconcilable gulf had yawned among the pioneer families which was to endure into the twentieth century.

The enlightened Samuel Spencer probably continued his ministrations around the Mira area until about 1853, in the course of which he sired nine children. Whether or not he ever received any theological training is unclear, but after that year, successive moves to Pictou and Cumberland Counties indicate his continuance as an itinerant preacher. Other Spencers were to follow in his footsteps.

Anthony's family, though, was to make the outstanding contribution toward passing on the "Word." Born in 1818 as the fifth son, Anthony junior attended Horton Academy for two years and, short of means to continue, taught school at North Sydney, preaching meanwhile in the homes of people in various parts of Cape Breton until his formal ordination in 1849. He has been described by a contemporary, evidently another clergyman, as "a man of noble physique, a commanding appearance, strong mind, a pleasing voice, a man with a deep and intimate knowledge of the sacred scriptures, a clear and definite grasp of the doctrines of grace, a man, indeed, to whom ministry listened with profit and delight."

At least two of the grandsons were also to become ordained ministers of the Baptist faith. The other five sons, including Arnold and Thomas, two of my great-grandfathers, maintained the faith in a less active way by settling down on their grants at Round Island in the role of fishermen-farmers. One of them, Charles, later evidently moved to Louisbourg and was killed in a railway accident in 1873 on the newly constructed Sydney and Louisbourg Railway.

Perhaps no family better illustrates the rapid expansion of relationships than that of Anthony and Lucinda: their six sons and six daughters ended up with 106 children, and the descendants of these in the next generation number well over 300. Numbered among the 106 were my grandmothers Adelaide, daughter of Arnold, who married Jane Lisby

Earle Peach's "tenuous link" to the past was through his grandmothers. Left to right: Mr. and Mrs. Theodore Martell (brother of Jane), Addie Peach with daughter Evelyn, Grandmother Adelaide Murrant, and Grandmother Jane Peach.

Huntington, member of another Loyalist family, born in 1837, and Jane Levina, daughter of Thomas and Susan Mehitable Martell, born in 1851. Thus by the latter date two of my grandparents were living at Round Island, and two, Thomas Peach and William Henry Murrant, lived at South Head, about seven miles distant. As both of the latter had died before my arrival, my very tenuous link with the past was to depend upon my grandmothers, both of whom survived into my teenage years.

Practically nothing is known of the lives of Arnold and Thomas Martell, except that both were fishermen-farmers, both lived at Round Island, and that in his later years Thomas was apparently involved in a large number of real-estate transactions around the area, a fact made evident in the Registry of Deeds. Between 1837 and 1857 Arnold and Jane raised a family of two sons, both of whom died in infancy, and six daughters, the eldest of whom was grandmother Adelaide. Between 1844 and 1866 Thomas and Susan Mehitable raised a family of five sons, only two of whom survived to marry and raise families, and five daughters, the second of whom, Jane Levina, born as a twin, became my grandmother Peach. After the death of his first wife on January 11, 1866, Thomas lost little time in remarrying, for on June 21 of the same year he was espoused to Sarah Spencer of Margaree, a marriage that was to produce another four daughters, thus giving him a total family of fourteen—a man of vigour indeed.

Meanwhile, in his bleak eyrie on South Head, James Peach and his unknown Margaret brought forth a family of two sons and four daughters. The elder son, John, married Susan Andrews and settled in

Port Morien to father a large family of sons whose descendants have multiplied enormously. The younger son, grandfather Thomas Peach, was also to leave the bitter site on South Head and raise a large family.

On the Murrant acres, on the less-exposed side of the head, Thomas Murrant, Jr., and Anne Boutilier came forth with three sons and five daughters, the eldest son of the family being grandfather William Henry. The three sons continued to live on the Murrant property, but as only one male grandchild from their marriages lived to maturity, and he failed to produce male issue, this branch of the family was to disappear.

Undoubtedly the most exotic of my ancestors, and likely the most entertaining, was Thomas Murrant. A sketch of family history, based largely on oral tradition and repeated by Thomas himself, follows. He was born in Fécamp, France, in 1787, and was educated, in his youth, for the Roman Catholic priesthood. Much to his family's displeasure, he renounced that faith and became a Huguenot. At age sixteen he was drafted into Napoleon's army to protect Flanders against the armies of England and Prussia. Still later, ostracized by his family and friends, he fled to England and entered the British Navy, where, because of his superior education, he became an officer on a man-of-war. To quote from family annals: "Following a conflict with a superior officer, because of his rebellious temperament, Murrant was put in irons and later lashed to the mast and whipped with the celebrated cat-o'-nine-tails then in use in the British Navy."

Let us examine this story critically. Thomas was sixteen at the time of his induction into the army; in 1803 Napoleon *was* anticipating an attack on the Flanders coast. The stories he used to tell of his hardships in various campaigns were accepted uncritically by those who knew him. Let us assume that at the time of his flight to England he was twenty-one. Although the British Navy would have taken on anything that could stand on two legs, it was more select in its choice of officer material, and he would need a few years to learn the language and prove his capability. At the time of his flight from the navy he must have been at least twenty-five, and the year 1808.

No respectable Loyalist widow with three children, like Orelia Payne Peters, was going to marry a "furriner" who had escaped from the navy until he had thoroughly proved himself in the community, and that took time. They were married not earlier than 1812 or 1813, for the first son was born in the latter year. Perhaps the most convincing factor of authenticity is that the marriage is not recorded in the annals of St. George's Anglican Church in Sydney, and for a very good reason—Thomas was still officially a fugitive! Their union either took place outside the church, or a sympathetic officiating clergyman just forgot to record it. Significantly, none of the six children born between 1813 and 1824 was reported in christening records, though all the grandchildren are found there, and Thomas's second marriage in 1847 is recorded. Up to that date the good Thomas is just a non-person. No land grant is assigned to him on early maps, though grants appear in his sons' names and in the name of his second wife. All these facts lend credence to his story.

In the Census of 1871, the first census of families, his eldest son, Thomas, one of my great-grandfathers, is shown to be of French origin, though his brother John, who settled in Big Glace Bay, is noted to be of German origin; perhaps a Murrant joke on the census taker or a bad guess on his part.

The Murrant grants on South Head lie about two miles east of the grant assigned to John Spencer and thus in a position more exposed to the gusty eastern gales. Only minimal farming, including the raising of sheep, was possible there, so Thomas, like his Peach contemporaries on the south side of the Head, took to the sea and fished. We can surmise that, as an educated man in a milieu of semi-illiterates, he was inclined to take advantage of this and to acquire in certain circles the reputation of being in league with the Dark Powers. Father used to relate that his grandfather James Peach was convinced of Thomas's wizardry; he could draw rum out of the mast of a ship at sea. Once, when Jim was visiting him, he took advantage of Tom's absence, at the shore a few hundred yards away, to look for his "black book." Sure enough, he found it and was about to open same when Tom miraculously materialized at his elbow and shouted, "Don't open that, Jim!" Because Jim was probably illiterate, we wonder at the story.

Another conjuration credited to him was the ability, when a friend was visiting him, to take a pack of cards, pick one, and say to the friend, "When you get home and open your door, this card will fall in front of you."

This aura of the supernatural was enjoyed not only by Thomas, but also by twenty-seven-year-old Catherine Sutherland, whom he married at the age of sixty. A Scottish girl, she, too, was to inherit the mantle. Old Kit Murrant became a person to be feared; likewise their only daughter, Catherine, who was living in my youth. The latter had married a Roman Catholic by the name of Clark, an unhappy alliance which soon left her alone. Early each Sunday morning she used to drive around the bay in her horse and wagon to attend mass in Port Morien. This alone, in the eyes of children with a strict Baptist upbringing, was enough to render her sinister and awe inspiring. When, on the odd occasion, she tethered her old horse in the yard and dropped in on her relatives for a cup of tea, we instinctively shrank into corners.

Three of the sons of Thomas and Orelia, Thomas, William, and Anthony, married and raised families of their own on South Head; John, as noted, moved to Big Glace Bay, where he raised a family of seven sons and two daughters. Great-grandfather Thomas was to marry Anne Boutilier, of whom little is known except in a general way. The Boutiliers, Waddens, Clements, Mileses, and Currys had derived from a regiment (RNIR) disbanded in Sydney shortly after 1800, and these families had settled on small parcels of land on the southern side of the Head. Here on the outer rim of Mira Bay, open to the unbridled fury of the Atlantic, little except a few miserable potatoes could be grown, and they eked out a bare existence by fishing when it was possible to launch their small boats into the bay.

A glance at the map shows that the western section of South Head is cut off by a sand bar from the outer reaches of Morien Bay. On the inner segment, where the Spencers, and later the Shepards, were to take up grants, successful diversified farming could be carried on, making these families less dependent upon the whims of the sea. East of the bar, thin clay soil, and an exposed position, rendered farming hazardous, while at the extreme end vegetation degenerated into short grasses interspersed with stunted, distorted spruce trees bent far over to the west by furious Atlantic gales.

The Murrant holdings lay about midway between the two extremes and directly across the bay from the present village of Port Morien. Sheep farming, as noted, could be their only practical supplement to fishing. In a pioneer economy, such an alternative was not be be scorned, for people had to clothe themselves, and the Murrant women, with their spinning wheels, handlooms, and mat frames, probably contributed as much to the general economy as did their husbands in their fishing boats. In fact, it is not too much to say that without their flocks of sheep no early pioneers could have survived the rigorous Cape Breton climate. What other animal could provide both food and clothing? Within my own memory our socks, sweaters, and other wearing apparel derived chiefly from the flocks on South Head.

Although in the beginning the site they had chosen, or drifted into, was vastly inferior to that of the Spencers and Shepards, as time went on, its advantages were to increase. In mid-century Cow Bay developed rapidly into one of the prime coal-shipping ports on the coast and contained a far larger population than it has today. Such an expanding market could only improve the fortunes of the fishermen-farmers of the area, who up to that time had seen little currency of any kind and had lived chiefly by barter. The log houses, heated by stone fireplaces, could now be replaced with those of sawed lumber and heated by coal stoves, with a cheap and abundant supply of fuel.

The Murrants, though, did not become even slightly prosperous. The "rebellious" and adventurous spirit of old Thomas seems somehow to have been lacking in his descendants, or to have become exhausted in struggles against a harsh environment. Little is known of the life of

Thomas junior, except that he and Anne Boutilier raised a family of three sons and five daughters, including my grandfather William Henry, who was later to marry Adelaide Martell. The family was plainly unperturbed by the religious mania that later engulfed so many of their neighbours, for though the burial place of Thomas senior is unknown (probably unmarked on his own property), Thomas junior and wife Anne were laid to rest in the little Anglican churchyard on the property of John Spencer, a stalwart defender of the Established Church.

Last Year of Freedom

Chapter Five

Let us now return to the twentieth century and the Peach homestead. To a four-year-old, even the fenced limits of my family's one-acre lot represented a huge and exciting world. Just outside the kitchen door the puddles that accumulated needed to be drained away with a sharp stick, apples fell off the yellow-transparent tree into the wet grass, the still warm eggs that the hens dropped into their nests, the cow and the pungent aroma of the stable, the smell of hay in the mow, the reek of fish and kerosene in the storehouse, the rise and fall of the tide in the brook—a thousand interesting sights, sounds, and smells. Even if an inborn territorial imperative were not operating, the constant reiteration, "Now don't go over the fence," confined you within a simple and secure universe, and you took it for granted that it would remain that way, that the same sun would come back tomorrow, that your parents and brothers and sisters would still be there, and that nothing could change. This was the land of lost content, the Eden without a serpent.

When you crawled through the bars of the fence, though, you entered a much less secure universe. Out in his pasture John Martell had set up a sawmill powered by an old steam "crusher engine" which puffed and panted and periodically gave forth a high-pitched, piercing whistle that could be heard for miles. People from all around hauled their logs here, to be sliced up into boards by the whizzing, whining saw. Fatal, forbidden fascination! This was a man's world with no place in it for kids, and when we ventured timidly into it, it soon became apparent that we weren't welcome. Neither John nor his sons employed delicacy and finesse in discouraging youthful curiosity. If rough language failed to do it, there was always recourse to a boot in the tail. Lock, stock, and barrel, I hated the Martells! And there were a lot of them to hate, for John had five sons and six daughters. The youngest son was my own age and of a rough, bullying disposition compared with my rather shrinking one. John was Father's first cousin, but as he and his family took little interest

For young Earle Peach, the world was huge and exciting, containing a thousand interesting sights, sounds, and smells.

in church affairs, and it was well known that he was not above taking a drink, within our household they rated merely as friendly foreigners, rather unpredictable people.

Once you had crossed John's pasture, though, a realm of infinite delight lay before you, the kingdom of my Uncle Tim Peach, who still made his living from the sea. When not fishing, he spent his time at home mending nets, making lobster traps, and building boats, and the most joyful days of my youth were to be spent literally in his footsteps. A kindly man who each Sunday morning droned through a word-by-word recital of the Sunday-school lesson, his only venture at reading, he seemed to enjoy my company, for his eldest son was grown up and the youngest still unborn. I can see him still, very brown and wizened by the sea, a constant drop threatening to fall from the end of his sharp nose as he steamed the bows in an old iron pipe and knit headings for his lobster traps. Though usually in a good humour, he was a very taciturn man. There was no need for conversation; the mere fact that he tolerated my childish attention and remarks was enough to make me love him more than my own father. Aunt Annie, too, was always ready to welcome a young nephew with an abundant supply of raisin cookies.

One winter he and his younger brother Tom undertook to build a large "whaleboat" for deep-sea fishing. This must have been fifty or sixty feet long with a draft of six or seven feet, a major enterprise considering that they themselves sawed all the lumber for it, built the model, and followed it to the letter until construction was complete and the ship emerged from its temporary shelter into the open field. Naturally, I had followed each step with wide-eyed interest and, in the process, had acquired a nautical vocabulary of impressive dimension.

An inveterate tease, Uncle Tom had an instinctive gift for wearing away a child's self-esteem. On the morning of my fifth birthday he presented me with a board game about eighteen inches square. On one side he had carefully drilled the pattern for a fox and goose game (somewhat like Chinese checkers), on the other the black-and-white squares for regular checkers. Naturally, I was more than delighted with the unexpected gift, upon which he had spent so much labour, but every rose had to have its thorn; printed in indelible ink on one side was the inscription "For Short-Legs." I swallowed my seething anger and vowed revenge.

One day, as my two uncles stood by to admire the work of art that had just emerged from its cocoon, my opportunity came. In a voice choked with devastating scorn, knowledgeable cynicism, and hope, I said, "Wouldn't I laugh if she went to windard!"

The huge guffaws of laughter that greeted my remark told me that once again I had missed the target, and I departed from the scene in the greatest discomfiture. Unfortunately the whole episode had to be relayed to all my relatives, to the accompaniment of additional gales of laughter. Uncle Tom was never to forget this. When I visited him a few years ago, after an interval of forty years, his welcoming remark, as I anticipated, was, "Wouldn't I laugh if she went to windard ... haw ... haw ... haw!" Only by then could I join in the laughter.

I am sure that I would have been quite content to continue in my role as consultant to my fishermen uncles for a much longer period, but this was not to be; as long as I could remember, my brother and sister had been "going to school." And at least once I had been dragged up to Homeville Church to see them participate in a school Christmas concert, in which my sister sang a song, and my brother gave a dramatic, stertorous performance as he laboriously emptied and classified the contents of his pockets—"more string ... enough to stake a cow!"

Thus at age five my good days were to come to an end. In my best

made-over clothes I was seized by the hand and dragged two miles up
the road to Homeville School with a bunch of kids of all ages who knew
me not. The bell rang, and I was poked into a hard seat a mile too big
for me, and all was quiet. Then some of them lined up in a row and tried
to read something from their books and tried to spell words the teacher
asked them. So that was what it was all about. Pretty damn dumb! I could
do that already, thanks to the old Enterprise stove and the old primer
used by my brother and sister, which I found very exciting. As I recall,
the first lesson (with illustration) was:

> Bang! Bang! Clang! Clang!
> Hear the gong.
> Here come the fire reels!
> The people are running.
> They are shouting, too.
> What is the matter?
> It is a fire.
> Hurry, hurry, noise and scurry,
> Hear the fire bells ring!
> To some a sport, to most a fear,
> A fire is a terrible thing.

The gripping intensity of such glorious lines far surpasses the pallid
exploits of a later Dick and Jane, even though seventy years later the
fire reels have yet to make an appearance in Black Brook and Homeville.
In recognition of my complete pre-knowledge of the primer, Miss
England, my first teacher, promoted me without further ado to Grade
Two, where, if my memory serves me, on page two or three I was to meet
with the charming "Little Sorrow," with illustration:

> Among the thistles on the hill
> In tears sat Little Sorrow;
> "I see a black cloud in the West;
> T'will surely rain tomorrow.
> And if it rains, where shall I be,
> And who will keep the rain from me?
> Woe's me," said Little Sorrow.

School Days

Chapter Six

As it would be pointless to attempt any chronology in the years that followed my introduction to Homeville School, I shall settle for a more general view of the period, reflecting as it does a situation little different from that of thousands of rural Canadian schools in the 1920s. Our dejected version of the "little red schoolhouse," which had sheltered our fathers for brief periods in the past, was a twenty-by-forty-foot structure with three small multipaned windows on each side, finished in gray weather-beaten shingles, and heated by a potbellied stove in the centre. To emphasize the position of authority, the teacher's desk sat on a raised platform at the front; to emphasize a difference between boys and girls, each entered by a separate door from the cloakroom at the front of the building, though they had to mingle freely inside.

Sanitation facilities included an ageless, beautiful spring a quarter-mile distant that flowed from under Homeville Ridge, from which the water pail was filled daily by the pupils on a rotating basis (a favoured chore, since it could be carried out on school time). Also the usual two-section privy in the woods next to the school, tastefully adorned with choice graffiti and stereotyped representations of male and female sexual organs.

If the school building was unattractive, its site, a half-mile from the nearest dwelling, could not have been chosen more happily for children. North across the highway ran the ridge, a steep, gravel accumulation a hundred feet high closely covered with spruce and balsam, along which, by leaping Tarzan-like from tree to tree, we could prolong an escape from dull Mother Earth. Both boys and girls were swingers of birches à la Robert Frost, and every young birch within a quarter-mile radius gradually became inclined from the perpendicular.

Directly across the road from the school a glacier had thoughtfully left a boulder of a ton weight that served as the home base for games of hide and seek. A winter adaptation of this game involved following

This was a typical one-room school in southeastern Cape Breton.

long trails through the snow-laden forest with the escapees trying to reach home before being sighted and shot at by the "law." Enterprising, youthful gunsmiths had designed zip guns that could fire .22-calibre bullets, which just fitted inside the pressure foot of an old sewing machine and were activated by a hammer off an antique musket. A more primitive version consisted of a small pipe plugged at one end, leaving a touch hole for lighting with a match. This device, loaded with powder and shot, operated somewhat erratically and offered much more danger to the gunman than to his intended victim. When detected, these offensive weapons were routinely confiscated by the teacher, and their lack of accuracy was enough to ensure that no one was shot, though it made the game more exciting. The chief victim of juvenile gunnery turned out to be the wainscotted ceiling above the potbellied stove, when during the teacher's absence at noon, heavy-calibre rifle shells were stood upright on the hot surface while all waited with covered ears for the mighty explosion.

Down a steep slope from the school, Marshall Holmes's abandoned farm provided an open playground for "stealing-caps" and random games played with rubber balls. Part of it was marshy and wet, but feet were seldom dry anyway, and in winter, especially after every recess or noon break, seats were dragged up around the glowing stove while we dried out. The rich pungency of this dehydration is beyond description, for some children had a change of clothes only when spring arrived. From our superior station in life, with typical childlike cruelty, we labelled them the "polecats" and tried to avoid sitting near them.

Tobacco was a rare commodity among the boys, but this did little to prevent smoking. Good cigarros could be made from carefully rolled birch leaves and small fern fronds, with which the area abounded. These could be wrapped in tissue paper from the copybooks to make very acceptable cigarettes, though this tinderlike material had a disconcerting habit of bursting into flames when puffed upon, and smokers could be identified by their burnt-off eyebrows, a concession to be made to manliness.

Considering the ingrown nature of the tiny communities served by the school, it is not surprising that practically all the pupils derived from the basic pioneer families. Among them were the three Peach families from Black Brook, the family of John Martell, the Esserys, grandchildren of James Martell, the family of Robert Spencer, a grandson of John, and from Homeville the McLeod family, grandchildren of Thomas Holmes. Although all were related in some way, as far as the children were concerned no relationship beyond the first-cousin level was recognized or even known about. For them the elders of the community existed only as models for mimicry. For some peculiar reason, derived perhaps from the custom of an earlier age, this whole generation of children, from the communities mentioned and from South Head, engaged in constant mimicry of the manners and speech of their "betters," and as will become apparent later, this droll habit had excellent sources to draw upon, for the elders were very unusual people of distinctive speech and customs.

Take for instance the "eel-spearing" game which we constantly played. Each winter the elders gathered on the ice of Homeville Lake, chopped holes through it, and prodded into the lake's murky depths with their double-jawed, single-pronged spears for the harvest of eels. They loved them. Consequently, every small pond within a mile of the school became for us a miniature Homeville Lake; with sharpened sticks we poked holes through the ice and fished for imaginary eels, all the while imitating and improvising with great dramatic skill the appropriate action and speech of the four elder Holmeses, Waddens, Tuttys, Spencers. In fact, one learned to walk the two miles from home to school and back entirely in the role he had chosen without ever deviating into his own speech. You could be Uncle Will or Uncle Tom (Holmes) for the whole day if you wished. I suspect that this native talent for drama ended with the coming of radio and a greater mobility. It survives today only in the very occasional meetings of those who participated in it fifty years ago.

In retrospect I have always puzzled over our musical fare in grade school. The songs we learned, such as "The Faded Coat of Blue," "Just Before the Battle, Mother," "Tenting Tonight," and many others, were plainly derived from the American Civil War, which indicated a considerable time lag. It was true, though, that we felt much closer ties with the "Boston States" than with a far-off abstraction known then as the Dominion of Canada. Sons and daughters of the third and fourth generations of Loyalists had returned in droves to the United States to seek employment and wider horizons; everyone had relatives there.

Another reason for our American songfest could be that our songbooks were of American origin and, like most of our textbooks, had not been revised in fifty years. Our geography textbook, I recall, gave the total population of the world as 500 million—this in the 1920s! A fond memory of this text is that I learned from it the rivers of British Columbia, for as listed, they had a lovely trochaic rhythm: Simpson, Finlay, Fraser, Thompson, Columbia, Skeena, Stickeen, and Liard. I was never to learn the rivers of Nova Scotia, but when in the late 1960s I visited British Columbia for the first time, I did so with smug, competent assurance. How many natives of that province could rhyme off the names of their rivers? In the course of time the irrelevant had become manifest.

Occasionally, when the skating was good and the need for a holiday had become overwhelming, we had a rather unique system of closing the school. After hiding in the woods on the previous evening until the teacher had left, we simply crawled in through a window and knocked down the stovepipe. Next morning we innocently walked two miles to find only a cold school, and because the damage could not be repaired that day, we were forthrightly dismissed. Other than this artifice, to be used only occasionally, our only hope for reprieve from a day of tedium lay with the weather. In the two-mile stretch between home and school lay three small streams spanned by pole bridges, any one of which in times of heavy rain could overflow and flood the road, sending us home hypocritically proclaiming that there was just no way we could get across.

If we except the annual visit of the departmental inspector, all responsibility for the education of two dozen children lay with the country schoolteacher; there was no one to say her nay. The only inspector I can recall was an elderly chap named Mr. Creelman, who made a pretense of quizzing us ferociously on a few piddling items we may have been expected to know. We viewed him with some disregard, for he usually smelled of liquor, and we knew he was Roman Catholic. He featured a disconcerting habit of whipping his horn-rimmed glasses on and off with such abandon that on one occasion they escaped from his grip and flew across the room, to his evident chagrin.

After Miss England, my first teacher, there followed two years with Miss Greta Spencer of Mira, an effective, lantern-jawed martinette. Sister Nettie, who by this time had secured a teaching diploma, filled in another year, one of double jeopardy, for if I misbehaved the news was relayed to Father the same evening and appropriate measures taken. Another teacher I have evidently forgotten. At age eleven, however, when, by skipping grades along the way, I had reached Grade Nine, a new and different era commenced.

Our teacher for that year was a Miss Henderson, from one of the Cape Breton towns and likely in her first year of teaching. Hazel, as she preferred to be called by her pupils, though by no means a beauty, fancied herself a replica of Nazimova, a screen goddess of the age, and acted accordingly. A slight girl with semi-reddish hair and a mole on one cheek from which tiny white hairs protruded, she lived in the world of movies and owned an enormous collection of movie-idol cards derived from the Sweet Caporal cigarettes she smoked. I can only conclude that Hazel was an early Cape Breton flapper, for it was the flapper age.

On returning from weekend visits to her home, she always proceeded to regale us with her experiences with boyfriends. At least a half-dozen of these were coaxing her to marry. I was by no means the oldest in the group, two or three were fifteen or sixteen, and with these she carried on a rather cute, coy relationship above my budding level of comprehension. She had a certain caprice in her moods, though, and on some days delighted in vigorous applications of the strap for very little reason. Early in the year, as she was returning from lunch at her boarding house, a half-mile distant, she espied a group of us stealing apples from an orchard not far from the school. Now, to steal apples from Arnold's orchard, a vacant property, had long been a school tradition, and we thought nothing of it. Nominally, though, the orchard formed part of the property of her old landlord, and to enforce this knowledge, she laid on to five or six of us with the strap ... my sole experience of being on the receiving end of corporal punishment, and believe me, I resented it. I felt it as a blot upon my escutcheon, especially as I had no respect for her anyway. Hence I was not exactly overcome with grief at the calamity that was soon to overtake her.

She was boarding with an elderly couple, descendants of the pioneer families and pillars of the Homeville Baptist Church. Their grandson, a husky lad who had spent a few months in the Canadian Army before the war ended, also lived with them, and it was rumoured that he and our teacher liked to take nature walks in the evening. Nothing much was made of this until an accumulation of snow had fallen, when young country sleuths detected strange and unusual patterns on the snowbanks, somehow reminiscent of a four-legged beast. Some deduced from this that the couple were just playing games in the snow, while others, wiser in the ways of lads and lasses, gave it a more delectable and exciting interpretation and resurrected verses of the old ballad "The Footprints on the Dashboard Upside Down."

In the post-Christmas season our teacher glowed with healthy romantic fervour, and her slight figure seemed to be filling out a bit, probably because of the good, hearty country fare. Later on, though, the fullness seemed to concentrate more in front, and she blushed when some of the boys made reference to this. By April, alas, word began to circulate around the community that Miss Henderson was going to have a baby.

In today's Sodom and Gomorrah such an event would elicit scarcely a ripple of interest; the teacher would finish her year, have her baby, and be back on duty in September. But in good Baptist Homeville in the early 1920s it seemed that Halley's comet had returned unexpectedly— shock, horror, and hushed tones. The good Holmeses were dismayed beyond belief, and Father, along with the two other trustees, was shaken by the catastrophe. What in the world to do? Lest her tender pupils should be infected by such immorality it was plain that Miss Henderson would have to go—and go she did. A local supply teacher finished her term. There were vague rumours later that to rescue his grandson from the toils of the law, her poor landlord had to fork out more than five hundred dollars, an enormous sum in those days. What became of Nazimova I haven't the slightest idea.

The incident, though, was to throw a chill on my scholastic career. Under her tutelage I was to gain my first acquaintance with French, Latin, algebra, and geometry, preparatory to writing Grade Nine provincial examinations at Port Morien. It turned out to be a complete disgrace; I became the first member of the family to fail a grade and was cast into outer darkness. My parents gave not the slightest consideration to the fact that it was anything but my own fault. But by September the fires had cooled a bit, another teacher had been engaged, and the prodigal son was allowed to creep back shamefully to school. There was to be no fooling around.

And indeed there was no fooling around. Miss Cameron, a mature, sedate young lady in her early twenties, was of the religious bent especially suited to our locality. The Hollywood and holiday atmosphere of the school came to an abrupt end, to be replaced by a regimen of hard work. By Christmas everybody in the school was eager to stay in late on Friday afternoons, to have Miss Cameron read to them selections from a book of religiously inspiring stories!

After a long career of teaching and supervising teachers, I think it only fitting at this point to pay a tribute to the *good* teacher and to call to mind how much so many individuals owe to the few they run across in the course of their schooling. I am happy to have known many who loved to teach and who under no circumstances would do anything else. Thousands enter the profession to make a living, and teacher's unions help to ensure that these are fittingly rewarded in coin of the realm. Only expressions of human gratitude can reward the outstanding teachers, and these we should not withhold. Within the limitations under which she performed, Miss Cameron was such a teacher; her only teaching aids were a kindly heart, the bounties of nature around her, and the feeling that it was her duty to see that children learned. And these were enough. If I did not pass my required subject "with flying colours," I at least made a credible showing, and this finished me forever with the dingy little school set in the woods below Homeville Ridge, with the dipper floating in the bucket of sparkling water filled each morning from the spring that gushed unfailingly from its base.

It would be pleasing to record that, having overcome this great hurdle, I was brimming with eagerness to face the next challenge, of entering Grade Ten in Port Morien High School, pleasing but distinctly untrue. I loathed the very thought of it and tried all summer to put it out of my mind, imagining all sorts of things which might happen to prevent it: I might get sick, the school might burn down, or maybe I could go back to Homeville and study on my own! Unfortunately none of these things was to transpire, and when dreaded September arrived, I set out alone on foot, a sad, sad hostage to Fortune. And this year Father had to pay a tuition fee of *ten dollars*! What a bloody mess life could develop into! Besides my brother and sister, no other boy or girl from Homeville school had ever gone any further. Why did this have to happen to me? Beneath his seemingly happy and carefree exterior lurked a deep, secret self-contempt for this stocky figure, with slightly protruding front teeth, just smart enough to seem never able to do anything right.

Halfway, on the three-mile walk to school, lay Morien sand bar, the abode of the MacDonalds (known locally as the Clams), whose pugilistic abilities were well known—Roman Catholics all. Willie, Tom, Newman, and Bernard all loved to fight at the drop of a hat. It would be like passing a dragon's den! Luckily on the first morning none was in sight, and I arrived, shaking, at Aunt Kate's home a little further on, whence cousin Tom Spencer, two or three years older than I and in Grade Eleven, was to guide my destiny. A slight, quiet, gruff character, Tom, I knew, feared neither man nor devil; from there on I would be secure.

The school at that time was a two-storey, many-windowed structure painted a repellent reddish-brown. It contained about seven classrooms of pupils from Grade One to Grade Eleven, a total of more than two hundred Protestants and Catholics. A frightening aggregation indeed! Grades Nine, Ten, and Eleven, occupying one classroom, were to be under the guidance of Miss MacKay (pronounced menacingly McKie), B.A., fresh from Dalhousie University. In her role as principal she was to become for me a new authority figure.

Whether or not Miss MacKay had had previous teaching experience I cannot say, but she had evidently arrived expecting discipline problems and was prepared to forestall them even before they had arisen. A short, plump figure with small, flushed cheeks and a voice whose pitch rose ominously with the slightest provocation, she never in two years, as far as I know, did relax in the aloofness displayed to the students in the school and to the teaching staff. Perhaps this was a defence mechanism to conceal a lack of self-confidence; if so it was reinforced by the zeal and delight with which she administered public strappings. Such events usually did not occur in her own classroom, where all and sundry were plainly terrified of her, but the whacks and wails among the lower echelons resounded through the corridors almost daily, at noon or recess. Miss MacKay was plainly a lady of the old school.

With a class of twenty-five in three grades, the possibility existed for only a minimum amount of actual teaching, so her *modus operandi* consisted of assigning and hearing lessons and checking homework, all of which she did conscientiously, remorselessly, and unfailingly. If you were assigned six pages in British history, you were expected to stand when called upon and recite word for word the contents of at least one topic heading in those pages. Failure to complete a geometry or algebra assignment could mean detention until five-thirty or later, which, as I was soon to discover, meant arriving home at six-thirty dispirited and weak with hunger. Under these conditions I was to rise to new heights of industry in completing my assignments, and though I was not to lead the class of nine or ten students, I could at least rank in the upper half and thus keep out of trouble, my basic aim. The only consolation to be found lay in the small library of literary classics from which one could borrow on weekends.

At age thirteen I found myself no more socially inclined than I was at age eleven; not for me the wild, hurly-burly of semi-rugby football in which many of the boys engaged at noon. This often ended with one pair of combatants in a fist fight encircled by all the students in the school and the arrival of the formidable Miss MacKay, whose burgeoning, high-octave rage never failed to daunt the most determined miscreant.

This does not mean, though, that I hid myself away in a corner to read books, for once I had overcome an initial reluctance to make new acquaintances, I found others, like myself, who were more introspective and reserved. It has often been said that considering its population and inaccessibility, Cape Breton has contributed more than its share of noteworthy citizens, and in miniature, this was confirmed by the students in Miss MacKay's classes. Layton Ferguson, son of the local county councillor, was later to become a well-known Glace Bay lawyer and M.L.A.; his brother Bruce became the provincial archivist, while Angus McQueen, son of a coal miner, later served some years as moderator of the United Church of Canada.

Oddly enough, the seating facilities in the school differed not a whit from those at Homeville—double seats bolted down to the floor. In the second year Layton and I sat together in the last seat in one row, and as fate would have it, immediately in front of us sat the chubby little maiden whose charms I had long been admiring from afar. At some point in this period it had slowly begun to dawn upon me that girls had certain characteristics which separated them from boys, and I had to feel a certain compunction and reservation in wrestling them around as we were accustomed to do.

About two-thirds along the route of my daily journey to Morien lived a fairly prosperous blacksmith. I had not been travelling the route very long before becoming aware that from his gate his daughters emerged each morning at the same time to head for school. Cousin Tom, a neighbour of theirs, and I were not long in learning their names; at times they even walked along with us. By the beginning of the second year, when Tom was no longer there, I had learned to time my itinerary to coincide with theirs and had become smitten with an absolutely dog-dumb affection for Joyce, the eldest. If chubby Joyce smiled at me or even in my direction, the whole day seemed to take on a new, brilliant suffusion of light. She had a lovely smile, but like *My Last Duchess,* "She liked what e'er she looked on and her smile went everywhere." I knew this and knew perfectly well that no girl in her right senses could possibly be attracted to an abject specimen of boyhood like myself but just to be in her presence seemed to suffice. Now this delectable creature had been placed in the seat immediately in front of me for the next ten months.

The irritating feature of this close association was that cool, reserved Layton, though seeming totally unimpressed by her girlish sallies, was always more vocal in reply to them than I, to whom each word and gesture seemed a jewel of inestimable worth. Her efforts, I am sure, were pointed more in his direction, and yet he was quite casual about them; but even when I did receive a morsel of attention, I still remained the "dull and middy-mettled fellow" who could summon up no brilliant or impressive reply. I was so completely involved with Hecuba that all words failed me, or like panting Venus left distraught by a youthful Adonis:

> So worse than Tantalus is her annoy,
> To clip Elysium and to lack her joy.

This dumb Romeo could picture himself in wedded bliss at some future time and conjure up unknown delights, an anticipation clouded with grave doubts, when, having secretly looked over the class register in Miss MacKay's absence, I discovered to my horror that Joyce was seventeen years old and I was only fourteen. Gad, what a shock! After all, a man could scarcely marry a woman *three* years older than he was! I was desolate and resigned for weeks. Such wild flights are probably common to many youths as they undergo the trials of puberty, and in later years, as a teacher, I often watched for such attachments in my classes, feeling sure that they existed. But a fourteen-year-old lad is a wary customer and seldom wears his heart upon his sleeve.

The *coup de grâce* to this one-sided liaison was administered by my cousin Charlie Shepard, who by some means or other had learned of my secret attachment. Charles was a few years older than I and infinitely wiser in the ways of women, hence I respected his opinion. When, under questioning, I numbly admitted my secret adoration of Joyce, he, without malice aforethought, airily ventured, "Ah, two fatties together. You'd make a nice couple." When the fatal import of this remark dawned upon my shattered consciousness, I knew it was no go; my ballooning dreams deflated in a flash, and I was left face to face with cold reality. She was not for me!

Stories of the Bridges

Chapter Seven

Not every small rural community had the distinct advantage of a central focus of interest such as Black Brook enjoyed—an old iron bridge that spanned a seventy-five-foot gap over the brook. How long it had existed I have no idea, but it was by no means the first bridge, for underneath it old wooden abutments remained from an earlier era. In the early years the clump, clump, clump of horse's hooves on this sounding board registered in every household, whereupon each woman in the community turned from her chores momentarily to gaze from the window to identify the passer-by, while children often raced out to shout at him.

Each evening the young invariably collected on the bridge to review events of the day, sing, wrestle the girls around, and to play betcha games of treading the narrow steel girders twenty feet above the roadway. Above my right eyebrow I still bear a scar received in a collision with a projecting bridge bolt, an accident that required a hasty trip to Port Morien for stitching. But this was an unusual event, for in spite of our trapeze acts on the bridge, and our constant activity in boats and water, few were injured and none drowned. Even when someone broke through thin ice in the winter and thrashed around madly in the icy current, others were always around to fish him out. True, our parents could relate that some years before, a young man had "got drownded" near the bridge, had been rolled in vain on a barrel, and had not "come to," but he had not belonged to the community, so as far as we were concerned, this did not count.

Even today the same old bridge remains in its pristine ugliness. But progress has altered the extremely sharp turn at its northern end, where many early autos failed to make the necessary steering adjustment and ended up in a six foot drop into the frog pond, thus eliminating the need of putting boards studded with nails in the wheel ruts to blow out their 75 lbs/in^2 tires, a measure taken entirely in a spirit of science and

Each evening children gathered at the bridge to wrestle, sing, and tread the iron girders.

research. After all, we did have to have a look at these things.

In yet another sense the bridge was the focal point of the community, for it involved about the only external relationship with an outside authority. Periodically it had to be painted, and on such occasions four or five bridge painters pitched their tents on the flat area where Uncle Tim and John Martell wintered their fishing boats. By the time they had scraped away the accumulated rust, painted it over with a coat of red primer paint, and applied a new coat of shining black, they had almost become community residents, for they had drawn upon it for their supply of milk, butter, and eggs. Young painters had flirted with the local girls, and a fine and exciting time had been had by all. When the task had been finished, and the tents folded up, everyone felt a distinct sense of loss and looked forward to the next painting.

At longer intervals the wear and tear of iron-shod hooves thinned the flooring to a point where it had to be replaced. While this task required less time, it imposed upon the Peaches and Martells one of the most trying periods of social conflict. Who was to get the cast-off planking from the bridge? The external authority was no longer interested in it, and justice demanded that it be equally apportioned. Not that anyone needed it, for it could be used only for kindlings, of which there was already a surplus, but each would have felt negligent and irresponsible if he did not get his just share; to do less would somehow diminish his male prerogative and machismo. So the first claimant on hand picked carefully over the debris and set aside what he considered his just share—say that was John Martell's. Uncle Ab then appeared on the scene, a man who always felt that perhaps he was entitled to a little more than the others and chose his lot accordingly. By the time Amos Martell, Uncle Tim, and Father reached the treasure, they usually felt that the others had been rather generous in the division and would diminish, to some extent, the allotments set aside by their brother and cousin. All hell would then break loose, and a reign of terror would ensue in which none of them would speak to the others for weeks, a severing in relations which naturally affected their children, whose family loyalty was instinctive.

At that time Uncle Ab, whose eldest son, Frank, was to be my boon companion of early days, still lived in the original Peach house about three hundred yards upstream. As the governor's third son, Uncle Ab was reputed to be the golden-headed boy and chief heir, thus later inheriting the "new house" nearer the highway, a bit of good fortune that in no way lessened his feeling of being put upon and his tendency to suspect his brothers of subtle double-dealing. A small, brown, wiry man, who, when laconic speech failed him in moments of crisis, ground his teeth together in frustration, Uncle Ab fought a continual rear-guard action. If he and Father cooperated in buying a side of beef, he had to receive the choicest cuts; if they cut fence poles together, he had to have first choice of the cut. His working life had been spent as a section hand on the Sydney and Louisbourg Railway in a party of four captained by George MacPherson. When the latter had to retire because of illness, Uncle Ab inherited his position, but the responsibilities weighed so heavily upon him that in a short time he was in a state of complete collapse and had to revert to his original status. Not everyone is fitted to decide what tie in a railroad should be replaced.

Amos Martell, a son of James, lived with his sister Martha Essery and her four children in their old home, while his brothers had immigrated to the United States. This place had an unending fascination for us. First of all, it was the best coasting spot in the area. From beside the house you could streak downhill, land on the frozen brook, and continue indefinitely. Upstream lay the site of the old grist mill, with the stones still beside it, and near this stood the largest tree for miles around, a gigantic poplar. Downstream a bit you could dig out from the bank masses of sedimentary fossils depicting the vegetation of millions of years ago (though not by Father's fundamentalist reckoning). And finally, Amos had built a rowboat which for years was to transport us, and the Essery children, out to the estuary where we left our clothes on a large ant-infested boulder when we went swimming.

As was only natural among children, this household presented something of a mystery to us, for on only one occasion that I can recall did the Essery father show his face in Black Brook. Where he lived or what he did, other than abandon his family to their uncle, is still unknown, and it is unlikely that he even contributed to their support. "Uncle Amos" was to be their real father and support. A small, tough man around Father's age, and like Father, a colliery carpenter, he was identified chiefly in our minds by his metallic, nasal speech. It was believed that he had a "silver palate" or a "rubber palate," which is obvious nonsense, and that this accounted for the nasal pitch which we imitated by pinching our nostrils together. But this substitute father was not to be trifled with, and he administered his semi-paternal role with severity and no nonsense. Of the neighbourhood families, the Essery boys, around the ages of my brother and me, were the only ones to bear bruises inflicted by way of discipline.

Very discreet gossip among the elders sometimes reflected on the relationship between the brother and sister, but it was to surface loudly only in the wild rantings of good Grandmother Peach in one of her rare, but periodic, mentally disturbed conditions which caused her to indulge in Ezekiel-like denunciations of neighbourhood sins, a probable revolt against austere puritanism. Also, neither brother nor sister attended the Baptist church in Homeville, which left a gulf yawning between them and the Peaches. True, they sometimes rowed across the bay to the little Anglican church on South Head, but not often enough to proclaim themselves among the Christian "saved."

In later years, after his sister's death, Amos married his boyhood sweetheart from Catalone, an elderly Scottish lady who became "Aunt Mary" to the whole neighbourhood, endearing herself to them through her genial kindness and her tendency to use the Gaelic word order when speaking English.

Although relationships among the fathers of the community and their families could deteriorate over such trifles as bridge planking, as a rule they were friendly enough to ensure a certain solidarity in outlook and opinion. Economically, none was much above the subsistence level, which eliminated any opportunity for one to look down upon the other. But this is a need, and needs must be supplied. As Alan Watts had observed, every Yin must have a Yang, every up a down, and every in an out. This native sociological and psychological deficiency was filled by the "Covers."

When Grandfather Tom had abandoned the grim site of his ancestral home on South Head for greener pastures, there had remained behind not only a score of other Peaches but also an assortment of Waddens, Mileses, and Boutiliers, remnants of the disbanded RNIR regiment in Sydney. The Murrants and Peaches had intermarried with some of these, but over the years they had continued to intermarry with each other, with a resulting degeneration in heredity, and had inherited or somehow acquired a "dis, dat, deese, dose" type of vocabulary, a factor quite sufficient to provide us with our "poor whites."

Many of the Covers were of an irascible nature and, conscious that they were being looked down upon, were on very alert guard against any denigration of their dignity and could imagine insults where none existed. One day, on the way home from school, we met the most hypersensitive of them all plodding along the highway with a long pair of hip boots dangling over his shoulder. Whereupon, from a safe distance, we turned and chanted, "Where's the rubber boots going with the man?"

It was enough. He dropped the boots like a shot and took after us. Our youthful energy soon outran him, but it was not to end there. At noon the next day he appeared at the school with rage quite unabated, rushed in before the startled teacher, and exploded in a single breath, "Werz da bugger wuz givin' me all da lip an' sass las' night wun I wuz comin' up da road wit' da boots on me back? By God, I'm gunna find out 'bout dis! I wuzn lowed ta do da lika dat wun I wenta school."

We were duly summoned before him in cowering innocence, but because he could identify no single individual as an object for his wrath, he stomped off as furious as ever. Another of the Covers, an elderly man who tilted his head wryly to one side when speaking, suffered from a nagging wife.

When an acquaintance inquired how they were getting along, he replied, "Oh, not too good. She tried to pizen me agin."

"What was it this time, carbolic acid?" he prompted.

"Carbolic acid? Why, I'm used to that! This time it was a fine, white powder sprinkled in me tabaccy on the mantel."

In reality there was nothing unusual about the touchiness of the Covers, for many residents of small communities went about with chips on their shoulders; the people of Gabarus were known as the "roosters," and it was widely rumoured that if you crowed at a native of Gabarus, you either had to fight or run. On the north side of the Island the Scottish Judiquers harboured a similar sensitivity.

One of the most delightful examples of local patriotism used to be related by "little Danny" MacDonald of Port Morien. It was the era of the Fenian raids, and a local military had assembled a company of local Cape Breton youths to drill on Morien sand bar. When the exercise had ended for the day, he shouted enthusiastically, "Now, everyone give a cheer for his country!" Young Angus rose magnificently to the occasion and roared, "Hurrah for Mira!"

The only prototype of our famous Black Brook bridge in the area was the one spanning the tidal Homeville River, which led from the lake into the headwaters of Morien Bay. During our school days we were to become goggle-eyed observers for many weeks of a great triumph in engineering—the actual physical removal of Homeville Bridge from its site. Thereby hangs a rather long tale, though what its moral is I am still uncertain.

When the news broke, I was twelve years old. A coal mine was to be opened on the peninsula, about a mile from the beach, in the Homeville area. A private consortium of investors known as the Hiawatha Coal Company were undertaking the venture. Who they were and who directed them, local yocals never learned, but that did not matter. The industrial age had reached Homeville, and everybody would be prosperous.

Certain problems arose early on, however. First of all, the mine site was located in a remote area. The nearest railway was at least four miles distant—the Sydney and Louisbourg line, owned by the Dominion Coal Company, which did not look kindly on competition. To get around the problem, the new company built a wide corduroy road through the swamps on the east side of the lake, a formidable task in pre-bulldozer days. This road connected with the dirt road near the iron bridge. The company hauled mine machinery over the bridge, and soon coal was being mined in Homeville.

They quickly discovered, however, that only an insignificant amount of coal could be hauled away by the trucks then available. If the project was to continue, the mine would have to have a connection by water. But to build a coal pier that could withstand the southeasterly storms of Mira Bay would cost a fortune. Before their eyes lay the only alternative—Homeville Lake, a quiet, peaceful harbour separated from Mira Bay by False Bay Beach, a seemingly insignificant obstacle. All that had to be done was, cut a passageway through the beach, and *voilà*, the lake would provide a natural harbour for shipping coal.

At this point, the story of the "drudge" begins—none of us ever called it a dredge.

Where it came from or how it got there I never learned, but early in the year, this monster suddenly appeared outside the beach. Perhaps I exaggerate, but I remember it being one hundred feet long, forty feet wide, and bearing an enormous crane. In its control room sat a huge genial Italian named Carlo who, rain or shine, would suddenly erupt, in a fine tenor voice, into "Addie Ma Bella Napoli, Addio, Addio" à la Caruso. But life for Carlo would not be a sweet song.

The tale that follows has a Conrad-like ring to it—the irresistible force against the immoveable object. As Carlo sang and manipulated the levers, the huge orange-segmented scoop ground its way into the coarse beach rocks and sand, obstacles that had existed for centuries. Excitement in Homeville rose to a feverish pitch; there would be a Homeville harbour.

Then came the familiar autumn storm. Towering breakers from the bay swept sand into the area behind the drudge, leaving it marooned and only a quarter of the way through the beach. Carlo stopped singing. The only way out was to go backwards, and within a few weeks he had chewed his way into the ocean. Needless to say, by this time the hopes and sympathies of the community were deeply involved in this defeat, for the drudge, this immense contraption of steel and wood powered by coal-fired boilers, represented the wave of the future. But this was not the end.

Engineers visiting the site of this Waterloo reached the logical conclusion that if a passage could not be cut through the beach from the outside, it should be fairly easy from the inside, protected from the menace of Atlantic storms. The only real problem was how to get the drudge into the lake. But yes, of course, there was Homeville River, that little tidal stream running into the lake from the headwaters of Morien Bay. They decided to take the drudge up the river.

Towed by a heavy tug, the drudge left the scene of the battle and reappeared a few days later between the sand bars of upper Morien Bay, having circumnavigated South Head. From that point on, its progress was somewhat slower. Now the drudge, under full cargo, drew at least twelve feet of water, while the channel had a maximum depth of only eight feet at high tide. Obviously, it would not be full steam ahead.

But we still had faith in the drudge. Despite its first defeat, it would not let us down—too much depended on it. Day in and day out, under Carlo's skilled manipulation, its huge cantilever arm moved up and down, piling mountains of wet mud on either side as it winched its way forward. There was no stopping the drudge. It could do anything.

By the time school reopened that fall, the drudge had reached the estuary of the river, beneath the Stetsons' pioneer farm, and was chewing its way upstream. Every lunch hour and after school we raced a mile in delirious joy to watch it, clouds of black smoke pouring from its stack, the clanking of cables and heavy gears, and the wild shouting of its operators. This was a boy's dream of Heaven, a behemoth in motion.

But then there was the bridge. In the monster's path stood the one-hundred-foot-long steel bridge, built in the nineteenth century. The engineers could never move the bridge. Even the drudge couldn't move the bridge. But eventually the supreme test arrived, and on that day all the boys played hooky from school.

Keeping a respectful distance to avoid clouts on the head and boots in the tail from the workmen, we stood around in open-mouthed awe, placing childish bets and watching the miracle happen. Heavy steel cables looped over the bridge at various points hummed and creaked with tension as winches took up the slack. Clouds of smoke whirled down from the stack, obscuring our view of the exultant Carlo, now in seventh heaven. And then it happened. The bridge rose painfully and reluctantly from its piers and swung for a moment in mid-air, then the huge cantilever arm swung cautiously on its base and eased the bridge down into MacKay's field on the west side of the river. The drudge had regained its reputation.

On the following day, after passing between the piers, the drudge just as easily picked up the bridge from the field and shuffled it back into place. No sweat. In another couple of days this gem of our admiration had entered the deep lake and was steaming comfortably toward the beach. Now things would happen.

But unfortunately things did not happen. In fact, the same thing happened as in the first attack from the outside. In spite of heavy protective pilings, by the time the drudge was halfway through the passage behind it, the passage had filled with sand, and it was again marooned. The dream was fading slowly. Carlo's singing stopped. Slowly and sadly the drudge retreated down the lake and was moored in deep water off Three Stick Point. And there it remains to this day.

The enormous expenditure the drudge incurred bankrupted the Hiawatha Coal Company, so funds were not available to rescue the drudge from the lake. For a year or two, watchmen kept an eye on it. Then they also disappeared, and the whole episode was forgotten. Alone and deserted, the drudge swung at its mooring, accumulating rust and barnacles. As leaks developed in the heavy planking, the drudge sank lower and lower into the lake. A final plunge left only the upper part of the cantilever arm protruding, like Excalibur, from the sea. Then, as its supporting cables rusted away, it, too, vanished beneath the waves.

So ended the drudge, but not the story. In the early 1930s an earthquake centred in the Atlantic canyons off eastern Newfoundland rattled the Maritime provinces from end to end. A resulting tidal wave swept the coast, doing enormous damage to fishery installations. It affected False Bay Beach and filled the lake with mountains of water, which, when escaping, cut a small channel through the beach at the end, far from the drudge's nemesis. Later storms enlarged the opening. By the irony of Fate, this beach has completely disappeared, and Homeville Lake has become Homeville Harbour. But coal has never again been mined in the area.

The Model T, the Radio, and the Wireless

Chapter Eight

I was almost four and one half years of age when the First World War began, hence my memories of it are diffuse and impressionistic. As colliery carpenter at No. 22 Colliery, Father daily brought home with him the *Sydney Post*, whose news was invariably read to the family. We knew there was a *war*, but our only cross-reference on this subject was a volume in Grandmother Murrant's possession on the Spanish-American War, the gallant story of Admiral Dewey's campaign in the Phillipines against the barbarous Spanish conquerors, well illustrated for the time. The Americans had won, and that was good!

Father was just past the age commonly required for military service and remained at his job, even working overtime, though he often talked of joining up. A cousin on each side of the family enlisted on coming of age, but neither reached active service. The only community resident to attain this status was George Martell, John's eldest son, and on Father his family were to lay the blame for what ensued: a tragedy, ironically enough, brought about by a woman's love for flowers.

A passionate devotee of house plants, Mother had found little scope for raising them in the tiny windows of the house and had persuaded Father to build a bay window on the south side of the living room. In the course of this construction, young George, an excellent carpenter, was called upon to assist him. By the time the task was completed, Father, a wild patriot, had talked George into enlisting. He reached France and, in one of the early gas attacks, got his lungs filled with chlorine and was sent home. Although by this time he had married an English war bride and produced a daughter, he never really recovered from his ordeal and died before reaching thirty, our only war casualty. It may be argued, of course, that George would have enlisted without Father's persuasion, and with a similar result, but the incident serves to show the web of fate in which we are all suspended and provides a weighty argument for not messing into other people's affairs.

I can recall the headlines set in inch-high type heralding the gain of a few hundred yards of territory at a cost of thousands of lives under the reckless and stupid leadership of prestige-seeking generals. But the age of illusion was still strong in our hearts, and in school we loved to sing, "While the 85th Battalion Marches Through Berlin" and "With the Bagpipes a Hummin' the 85th's Coming from the Land Where the Maple Grows." On still evenings we could hear the band playing at Broughton, a few miles away, where a military unit was stationed. A member of one of these units had died there, and one afternoon we were released from school to stand around awe-struck as two or three hundred soldiers marched in full panoply and military slapdash to the Baptist church at Homeville and discharged their rifles over his grave. The empty brass cartridges became highly prized souvenirs in our childish war games.

Then came the Monday morning in November when it was all over. Although we expected it to be a holiday, we went to school anyway, joyously proclaiming the good news to all we met. One of these chanced to be Old Alonzo Wadden with his horse and wagon en route to Glace Bay. When we shrieked in a chorus, "The War is over, Mr. Wadden," his reply provided, in historical context, a comment more pertinent and incisive than the vast proliferation of books that were soon to flood the world's libraries: "Da war is over, is it?"

If our community had escaped most of the impact of that war, it was to be completely revolutionized by the developments which followed fast upon its ending. Apart from the fact that Father was supporting his family from his wages as a day labourer, previous to 1920 our lives were essentially the same as his grandfather's had been. Our little corner was so remote from the rest of the world that we were totally unaware of its existence. Glace Bay and Sydney represented the limits of knowledge, and visits to these, especially by children, were exceedingly rare and memorable. All this was to change overnight in the wake of the automobile.

As we were a horseless family, up to 1919 at least, the Peaches travelled on foot; even a train trip involved a two-mile walk to and from the station, and these were few and far between. To be pitchforked from this primitive state into the industrial revolution of the twentieth century was a very shattering experience, and one from which there was no return.

Father's overtime shifts, and a careful husbanding of resources, had placed him in the enviable position of being able to plunk down one thousand dollars in cold cash on the sales desk of Bezanson Motors in Glace Bay, and return home with a new Model T Ford. True, cousin Everett had got himself a Model T the previous year, but it was several years old, looked scrappy, and had to be cranked to start. Ours was brand spanking new, self-starting, and had snap-on isinglass side curtains! And

Sanford Peach brought home a brand-new Model T in 1919.

it *smelled* so good! We felt that Henry Ford had made it especially for us.

Where were we to keep it? The only building large enough to contain it was obviously the storehouse, where we kept the fish and supplies, but this meant that a new opening, with large, swinging doors had to be constructed in its front. This was done and we had our garage (a new French word), a new holy of holies. A new storehouse had to be constructed and this was also done. We were now the elite. Many a day I was to enter the garage, close the door carefully, and revel in the smell of gasoline and leather. It was the dawn of a new age, and life was good.

Probably the greatest impact was to register on Father himself. A small, lean man, clean-shaven and upright, he was suddenly to blossom forth in the black derby and brown jacket that were to grace the next forty-odd years of his life. When he sat behind the wheel with Mother beside him and slowly depressed the low-gear pedal, you sensed that here was a man of authority, a man who mattered, the only one of the Peach brothers to accept the challenge of the age.

Owning such a magnificent vehicle, though, entailed great responsibilities. In winter it had to be put up carefully on blocks, have its tires and other detachable items removed, especially the four spark coils and plugs, and all loose objects stored in the attic over the kitchen, to be reassembled in the spring. The year-round, you had to keep those spark plugs clean, especially No. 1, for it was common knowledge that all Model Ts threw oil from the base on No. 1, and if you didn't keep it clean, you ran on three cylinders. When on holidays we "looped the loop" through Glace Bay, Sydney, Mira Ferry, Mira Gut, and home, at least three stops would be required to clean No. 1 in this enormous circuit of forty miles. This was not in any sense regarded as a handicap, for it merely displayed the high degree of technical skill which the owner possessed. He was proud to do it.

In a year or two, as a special mark of esteem and confidence, I was allowed to clean the spark plugs occasionally, and once, in the performance of this duty, I incurred paternal wrath beyond measure. Preliminary to driving home the Reverend Mr. Ballard, Presbyterian clergyman of Port Morien, who had preached at Homeville that Sunday and later dined with us, I was sent out to clean the plugs. In the course of my new-found expertise, I contrived to drop the little nut from one plug down the hole into the cylinder. If I had violated a virgin, Father's rage could not have been more devastating. He drove me from the scene with an application of his boot, this on Sunday, and in the presence of a clergyman! My resentment against this loss of face was to smoulder for years, but it probably taught me a lesson.

Once we had become mobile, completely new vistas suddenly opened up before us. The little world encompassed within a two-mile radius, the world of streams, trees, and rocks began to recede into the background. In ten minutes we could be in Port Morien or Homeville, in a half-hour in Glace Bay, in an hour in Sydney. In a year or two we were making trips to Grand Narrows, St. Peters, and Baddeck.

Looking back upon this change, unemotionally from a distance, I have a deep suspicion that this was not an unmixed blessing. A nagging conviction stays with me, that each human being was destined to have a complete knowledge of and association with one very small part of the earth which he could call home. Perhaps the recruit on the sand bar was right when he shouted, "Hurrah for Mira."

One's native land cannot stretch *A mari usque ad mare*; the present divisiveness of Canada well illustrates the point. For many people the native land has to be a small place, a place that cannot be found by stepping out of an apartment on to a concrete sidewalk or by flying over seas and continents in jumbo jets. One's feet should never stray far from the muddy, dusty, pliant earth, and so convinced have I been of this that with the exception of one miserable four-year stint in Montreal, I have contrived, come what may, to keep my feet in contact with the soil, the old imperishable earth that even time cannot remove.

For this reason, too, on a recent visit to southern Portugal I found it comforting and reassuring to see the rural people riding along the highways in their horse and carts or perched casually side-saddle on their laden donkeys, while 150 miles away, in traffic-mad Lisbon, their compatriots searched vainly for a vacant sidewalk on which to park their cars, or waited patiently to dash across congested streets choked with gasoline fumes. But no politician, Canadian or otherwise, would dare to campaign on any other platform than that of progress; people must have more cars, skidoos, motorboats, super highways, colour TVs, and highrise apartments, and in order to achieve such lofty aims, they must be consumers, and if they are not consumers they must be converted, by hook or by crook, into consumers if the GNP is to continue to rise.

While the advent of the automobile may have broadened the individual horizons of small-community dwellers, it certainly exerted no unifying effect upon them; the net result was to be in the opposite direction, undermining their mutual interdependence by widening their choice of associates, just as it does today. The unifying bond of the 1920s was to be the telephone.

Early in that decade our community was swept up by the greatest joint endeavour in its history: the formation of the Homeville Mutual Telephone Company. As someone once remarked, nothing is as powerful as an idea whose time has come, and this was such an idea. I cannot recall if any one individual more than another was responsible for our entry upon the new age of communication, but the first organizational meeting was held in Sandy Peach's garage, as were most of the subsequent ones, so I may claim to have been present at the birth of this great enterprise. It meant that on meeting night the Ford was parked in the yard, and chairs from the house and innumerable boxes and barrels were placed in the garage for the Founding Fathers. Hither came such community pillars as Hen Munroe, Darcy Bown, Alex McIsaac, Amos and John Martell, Rob Spencer, Ronnie Holmes, Adam Kelly, Tom and Will Holmes, the Tutty Brothers, Stephen Wadden and, of course, the other Peach brothers.

At the very first meeting Father was chosen secretary-treasurer of the fledgling organization and was to continue in that capacity for the next ten or twelve years. As I recall, each prospective member was to contribute the sum of fifty dollars, to cut and install his just share of the total mainline poles, and to assist at the proper time in fastening the wires to them. Any extraneous expenses were to be borne by the Maritime Telegraph and Telephone Company, which hoped to recover its investment in the form of tolls.

It would be too much to assume that eighteen human beings, regardless of their mutual interest, could meet together for any reason without the usual bickering, arguing, and recrimination in which each tries to out shout the others, and with some threatening to become dropouts. Looking back upon it from quite a few years of dealing with the public, I can only conclude that Father possessed a higher degree of patience and diplomatic skill than he often displayed in relation to his own family. In his inimitable spelling, he kept the minutes of the meetings, did all the necessary correspondence and ordering of equipment, and smoothed over the rough spots as they arose. If he did not originate the idea, he, more than any other, must be credited with its successful execution.

In time, there arrived in our yard about twelve miles of wire, dozens of boxes of glass insulators, hundreds of brackets, and about twenty telephones, all supplied by the Northern Electric Company. By this time the post holes had been dug and the posts installed. Saturdays were spent stringing the wires. As each elongated wall phone, with its accompanying lightning arrester, was attached to the wall, the member verified the effectiveness of his equipment by ringing six rings, Sandy Peach's assigned number. Soon all were linked together.

By depressing a button on the side of the phone and cranking vigorously, it was now possible to connect with Central in Port Morien and thence, in rare cases, to contact Sydney or Glace Bay. The doctor could be summoned in emergencies, grocery orders could be phoned in to Port Morien.

Its real value, however, lay in its social cement. Now anybody's business was everybody's business. When in a year or two the line was extended to South Head and four more phones added, it meant that any routine conversation between two phone stations was often monitored by about sixteen other phones manned by listeners. One middle-aged subscriber was now able to have intimate talks with her mother, who lived five miles distant. Her father at this period was unfortunately elderly and ailing, and the conversations dealt in the utmost detail with his daily routine and symptomatic behaviour. In a society where mimicry was a natural talent, some of my female cousins soon adapted to this source of daily drama and could reproduce reams of such conversations, ad libbing to intensify the effect. Even today these ladies can reproduce word for word, in familiar accents, the more salacious details heard on the Homeville Mutual almost fifty years ago.

Inevitably the younger generation soon became prime users of the telephone, and perfectly aware that all conversations were monitored, some of us were not slow in conducting pre-arranged conversations filled with details of imaginary events of local interest and juicy gossip, which often created a high degree of consternation in the community. By monitoring in turn the next few calls, it was always possible to estimate the acceptance of these ventures as the "news" spread around the area, all of which served to make life more interesting.

As secretary-treasurer it devolved upon Father to inform each subscriber of his monthly charges in tolls and to see that they were paid. The monthly service charge was twenty-five cents, and each month the Maritime Telegraph and Telephone Company mailed him a total statement from which he compiled the individual bills and phoned the results to each customer. In the Peach household, "giving out the tolls" each month soon became a painful and enervating experience, not well calculated to win friends and influence people who often took the attitude that they were being exploited by the Peaches, who as far as I can recall, received no remuneration for this service.

The tolls were paid at our house, and this, too, sometimes led to complications, for Old Ben Wadden liked to pay his tolls on his way back from Glace Bay when he was well "lickered up." On one occasion he left his old Model T running beside the highway and arrived at the door to proclaim, "Sandy, I want to fight a Peach."

To divert his attention, Father suggested, "Ben, you know you left your engine running out there. Your car might run away on you."

Ben looked at him craftily from under his beetling eyebrows and replied, "Sandy, I want you to know that when I stop my car, she's stopped."

Sometimes when telephone wires became snarled in winter storms, semi-legal complications arose. Once, the lines had all been cleared, with the exception of Rob Spencer's (who lived a half-mile from the mainline). As Rob and his sons did not display sufficient zeal in effecting repairs, Father took it upon himself to snip off the Spencer line from the trunk line. Judge the outrage when this indignity was discovered! The incident served to darken for months our relations with the Spencers.

Close upon the modernizing thrust of the telephone came the astounding news that voices and other sounds could now be heard by "wireless." The wireless idea was not exactly new to us, for Marconi had used Table Head, at Glace Bay, in his early experiments, and from our kitchen window we could see the "Marconi Towers" four or five miles away. From these mysterious towers, thrusting hundreds of feet into the sky, we knew that messages were sent and received in code from all over the world. This was a kind of black magic which no one pretended to understand—except my cousin George Spencer.

Working from information derived from early magazines, he had devised a crystal set which, when fed from an antenna seventy-five feet high and one hundred feet long, produced voices and music from the eastern United States. Springfield, Schenectady, and even Pittsburgh could be identified in the close-fitting earphones. George and some of his friends even listened to the Dempsey-Carpenter prize fight, probably the first sports event to be broadcast. But at such distances the crystal set was unreliable and tricky. Its successor, the "vacuum tube," was almost immediately on the way in our locality.

Robbie Holmes, Uncle Will's son, had spent years in the United States as an electrician and, in spare moments from his successful fox farm, had been keeping up with new developments. Soon a long, high aerial blossomed over the ancestral home, and attached to its lead-in lay a weird

Goldbergian conglomeration of instruments known as variometers, variocouplers, transformers, condensers, and "peanut tubes." When the ten dials on the front of this awesome machine were successfully manipulated by the mastermind, the volume of sound was most impressive. Even Uncle Will could hear it.

To make a long story short, my brother and I wangled an invitation to visit Robbie's wireless. After a two-mile walk at night we crept into the "room" and donned earphones to hear an evening-long program of chorus selections and piano solos from WGY Schenectady. One did not quarrel then about programming, and commercials were completely undreamed of. It was a lovely and intriguing world, and it lies only sixty years in the past.

In a year or two the "raddio," as Rob called it, became more sophisticated and common. Father ordered a manufactured set from Montreal which had only six controls on its shining bakelite panel and proclaimed itself to be a Reinartz Regenerative Circuit, complete with three WD 11 tubes and three sets of earphones, which, of course, could be detached to serve six listeners. The most trying feature of the old regenerative set lay in its ability to transmit signals as well as to receive them, and as this type multiplied in the vicinity, the shrieks and howls in the headphones beggared all description. On at least one occasion I was to experiment in producing some competing interference.

I had been reading, in the early history of the wireless, that the original sound transmitted had been produced by means of large induction coils connected to a spark gap. It so happened that the spark coils from the Model T were then stored in the kitchen attic, and having obtained one, I proceeded to ground one side of the gap and connect a small aerial to the other. Meanwhile, Father, in the next room, had settled down with pipe, newspaper, and headphones to enjoy an evening's relaxation. When my signal came on the air, I heard his chair scraping back on the floor, so I paused for a while. Then at intervals I pressed the button again. In a minute he called loudly, "Earle, come in here. Something is tearing the guts out of this machine."

I went in very innocently, after asking Cousin Frank, my collaborator, to give it a shot while I was investigating; the blast in the earphones could have shattered an eardrum. I made a few adjustments on the dials and, lo, all was normal again; the noise was never repeated, and Father never learned the cause of it.

The old Reinartz went on for years, headphones eventually being supplemented by a cone-shaped speaker attached to the wall. Soon the long-distance reception craze was on, each operator vying with the other in receiving distant stations. I recall getting up at three-thirty in the morning. to pick up KGO at Oakland, California, and verifying the program. Later on I built a short-wave converter which, when attached to the radio, enabled us to pick up daytime programs from Britain and Germany.

A good many years passed before a local radio station made its appearance, and all our reception came from the eastern United States, which seemed quite normal. Our ties with this area even before this were much more evident than any kinship with the rest of Canada, and I have no doubt even today that the Americans who are buying up property in Cape Breton receive a warmer welcome than if they came from Quebec or Ontario. It is not that Cape Bretoners feel "left out" of Confederation; it is just that they feel they were never "in."

Music

Chapter Nine

As far as I can recall, none of the Murrants or Martells was noted for his musical talents or was especially interested in music, while most of the Peaches that I knew liked to sing, and this is still true of them today. We were most fortunate in this respect; for somewhere along the line, Mother had taken a "quarter" in music, and in his heyday, Father was gifted with a fine tenor voice. The one luxury item in our home was the old pedal organ in the parlour, around which each Sunday evening the family gathered to sing devotional and inspirational hymns. As a result, the whole family learned to sing and to improvise harmony. Because it was not easy for a group to follow the words from a single book, I found it an advantage to memorize them, and even yet I could compile from memory enough of these treasures of fundamentalism to fill several hymnaries. Although I have wandered far from the sentiments they express, they still have a habit of insinuating themselves into my consciousness each morning when I wake. I sometimes wonder what could be made of this.

As time went by, our repertoire became more secular; Father bought an accordion and wore it out in six months by playing, "Anybody Here See Kelly, Kelly with the Green Necktie?" The next adventure was the purchase of a "fiddle" made by a Hungarian miner for a price of ten dollars. Father and two of his sons became sufficiently skilled on this instrument to play "Redwing," "The Mocking Bird," "Over the Waves," and not very impressive renditions of "The Irish Washerwoman" and "The Fisherman's Hornpipe." Later someone left this valuable instrument lying on a chair in the parlour and someone else inadvertently sat on it. Like the Harp of Tara's Halls, its soul was shed.

In the twenties, ukuleles came suddenly into their own, and in a vigorous sales campaign I sold enough Easter cards to acquire one of these treasures, but what I really wanted was a guitar; at a crucial moment in one of Ralph Connor's novels the hero, swept by emotions far beyond his control, had sung an entrancing and most romantic air to his beloved as he picked the strings of his guitar. There was no way out, I had to have one, but this was beyond the range of postcard promotions in our area and before the days of "allowances."

At various times in life I have found that if things just *have* to happen they will happen, or as Macbeth put it more succinctly, "If chance will have me King, why chance may crown me without my stir." An unwise attitude no doubt, for chance usually needs a little nudging. In this situation, however, it was to operate entirely on its own; strolling through the woods one day, gun in hand, I came upon the body of a beautiful red fox, whose throat had been torn, probably by a rival, its pelt otherwise intact. I swung it by its gorgeous tail over my shoulder and headed for home, a fox-raising neighbour skinned and stretched it for me, sent it to his shipper, and not long after, I received the fabulous sum of seventeen dollars. I could get a guitar for fifteen, so this windfall put me in the Ralph Connor class with still uninvested capital.

The twenties were also the dawn of "Highwayan" music, that weird wailing of strings characteristic of the romantic isles of the blest; by the simple addition of a steel nut across its upper neck my treasure could be converted into an instrument straight from Honolulu, and after assiduous practice, my brother Harold and I were to become local celebrities with our guitar and ukulele combo; we even reached the supreme height of playing in public in Port Morien!

The superlative role of the guitar, though, lay in its "Spanish" chording possibilities. Although unlisted in Pete Seeger's catalogue of balladeers, Vernon Dalhart must have been one of the first to get this type of singing on disc. His plaintive songs of train wrecks, lonely cowboys, remorseful convicts, and lovers separated by death, all set down on fast-spinning 78-rpm discs, set a style that lasted for years. No tricky, razzle-dazzle rhythms for Vernon, he played it straight from the cuff, with the thumb picking the bass strings and the first three fingers picking suitable major chords, the sort of thing Ralph Connor had in mind. Vernon's style became my style, and thus it has remained. For years it occurred to no one that the guitar had any other possibilities, until in the fifties it began to acquire fame as the instrumental accompaniment for personal protest and subjective expression. Now each balladeer has to have his or her individual style of feathering intricate chord patterns and rhythms, and even the classical guitar has come into its own.

But nothing so far has surpassed the old 1920 style for conducting singsongs, and over the years this has remained my delight. Regardless of location or circumstance, one always runs across people who like to sing, and for me it is a sick party indeed without the old songs of tragedy, brave engineers, lonely cowboys, and the strident uplift of the old gospel hymns, suitably interspersed with pauses for refreshment.

Up to the advent of radio our only experience with music, other than the home-produced variety, came from the gramophone. We were never to own one of these, but Uncle Clyde, who lived with Grandmother Peach in the new house, had by my time acquired an early Edison featuring a huge horn attached to a relatively small "works," which used the early dictaphone-style cylindrical rolls. As it was the only one in the immediate neighbourhood, when operating it, he felt all the beaming pride of Moses striking water from the rock. On special occasions Father or Mother or both might take us to listen to this amazing contraption if we promised to be good.

Being good, of course, meant sitting immobile with hands folded while Uncle Clyde, in his infinite skills, manipulated the awesome controls and produced sound. It was as well not to be too near him, for a chronic catarrhal condition and the medicaments with which he treated it gave him an overpowering breath. His well-known tendency to erupt suddenly into alarming epileptic fits also made one wary (this had on occasion occurred in church, much to the consternation and distress of his relatives).

As master of ceremonies he casually selected a cardboard-enclosed cylinder, drew it cautiously from its container, slid it over the receptacle, teased its surface with a little brush as it revolved, turned the mechanism which lowered the needle on the record surface, then sat back with all the gleeful pride of a Cheshire cat. Following a scratchy prelude, from the cavernous recess of the big horn emerged the reedy tones of an orchestral introduction, then the spectral voice of Henry Burr singing gospel hymns or on week days those of Ada Jones and Billy Murray singing a naughty, "I've Taken Quite a Fancy to You, Dear; I'd Like to Paddle Your Canoe." Although he was to remain a perennial bachelor, Uncle Clyde always convulsed with glee when he heard this number, especially the lines, "There's no one in this wide, wide world, dear, whose tootsy-wootsy I would be, if you'd only take a fancy, dearest, to a fancy little [boy-girl] like me." Alas for sophistication!

A mile along the road to Homeville lived Ronnie Holmes, the next proud possessor of a talking machine, but this was a real Victrola that used flat discs. On rare occasions we were taken to hear this new wonder, the pride of his sister Kate. Kate was generally recognized to be a "lady," a more highly cultured type than was common, which did not necessarily endear her to a community that scorned culture and all its works. Thus the Holmeses' repertoire featured some McCormick recordings and operatic selections, though Ronnie, a hearty down-to-earth type who always smelled of cow manure, enjoyed above all his wide selection of "Cohen" records—"Cohen at the Dentist's," "Cohen and the Carpenter," "Cohen and his Auto"—all of which never failed to arouse gales of laughter with each hearing. The Jewish dialect slowly worked its way into our dramatizations of local notables.

The full cultural impact of the phonograph, though, was to manifest itself upon Ernie Shepard, Uncle Ab's brother-in-law who, along with an up-to-date Victrola, had acquired a wide selection of Caruso recordings, to which he not only listened but applied himself diligently to memorizing in Italian, of which he understood not a word. Gifted with an excellent high-tenor voice, his renditions of the immortal Enrico were nothing to be ashamed of, especially at our night-time skating parties. It was not easy to get him started, but once under way he skated in ever-widening circles around the bonfire, pouring forth his soul in operatic fervour. It would be pleasant to recall that such a cultural triumph used to receive our enthusiastic applause, pleasant, but untrue, and such variations from the norm were rewarded only with suppressed snickers.

Many years later, in a search for early Caruso recordings, I visited him at his old home, where he lived with his dog in the utmost squalor. His record collection was still intact but piled under heaps of debris and filth, scratched beyond recognition. Sure, I could have had them, but they were not worth taking. He had not sung in years. He could not even remember when he had sung. Ernie had been a flower that was born to blush unseen, and somehow this seemed a great tragedy.

The Seasons

Chapter Ten

Only a person who has spent half a lifetime in each place can adequately assess the contrast in climate between Cape Breton and central Canada. In the latter, winter changes into summer so rapidly one is scarcely aware of a season called Spring. Winters of course are much colder, but with a dry cold that nips rather than penetrates. When the snow has gone, usually by the end of March, green grass and swelling buds are not far off. Temperatures of eighty degrees in May are not uncommon, while such a temperature in Cape Breton at any time is considered a heatwave.

An easy comparison between the two would be to say that the Ottawa area experiences about three months more shirt-sleeve weather than does Sydney, for which Maritimers can thank the Labrador Current with its drift ice, which arrives in January and can hang around as late as the May 24. The damp, bone-chilling cold of these five months still weighs upon my earliest memories.

After the last "clampers" of drift ice had trailed out of the bay on an ebb tide, a slow, never-ending spring crept in silently under the masking fog. As I shivered in bed at night, I heard the long drawn out boom of the siren on Flint Island, followed by a faint, gruff answering echo from the foghorn at Mainadieu, on Mira Bay, and remembered Grandmother's stories of the Martell sea captains who had never returned from voyages; in one of them, in 1899, most of the sons of two families disappeared.

When late afternoon suns had chewed away the snow, in between the puddles on the hills at Deep Cove, masses of mayflowers (trailing arbutus) emerged, tiny, pink blooms of exquisite scent native to the Maritimes. On Arbour Day, as children, we spent the morning tidying up the school and grounds and got the whole afternoon off to pick mayflowers, some of which were taken home to mothers, while the remainder came back to school the next morning to be shyly presented by scrubby hands to the teacher.

No sooner had school closed than the berry-picking season was upon us. First came wild strawberries, the tiny, elusive red fruit that hid in the deep grass and took so long to pick and hull, and settled down in the basket so fast that you could never get the bottom covered. In spite of this, Mother packed lunches for her current crop of chickens and herded them out to the wilds at the wash plant; nowhere else were the berries so large and so plentiful, for they seemed to have an affinity for coal ash.

The prospect of this expedition was by no means as gloomy as it should have seemed, for the wash plant was another place of infinite delight. Strewn around haphazardly among clumps of fluttering aspens lay the old, rusty machinery once used in the coal-washing process, all of which merited close attention. Its fascination paled into insignificance, though, compared with the feature attraction; through this area stretched the gleaming rails of the Sydney and Louisbourg Railway, bordered on either side by high telegraph poles holding masses of wires that sang in the wind. You could put an ear against one of these poles and hear thousands of messages being sent over the wires.

The supreme thrill, was to hear the shriek of an approaching train with its long string of coal cars; clouds of smoke and steam heralded the arrival of this Chariot of the Gods, its metal glistening in the sunlight. As it drew near, we could see the engineer casually poking his head out the cab window, and if this master of destiny condescended to wave to us, our cup overflowed. Sister Nettie always grumbled that I used this thrill as a ruse to escape picking berries, but she was being petty; my open-mouthed admiration transcended the very existence of strawberries. Any boy in the neighbourhood could identify any locomotive by number just by hearing its whistle. Numbers 58 and 59 were the really big coal haulers; No. 23, the fast express that tore down the grade toward Beaver Dam each morning at ten o'clock. Some boys could even identify the engineer from the way he handled the whistle, though this could lead to endless arguments with the boy whose uncle was a "real fireman."

Then came the annual pilgrimage to the "bakeapple barren," about a mile distant. In July this square mile of steamy peat bog became dotted randomly with single stems bearing the composite berry known only to connoisseurs of Cape Breton and Newfoundland fare, the most delicious berry of all. Hard, pink, and golden at first, it soon ripens into a soft, mouth-watering yellow blob of indescribable flavour. A day spent traversing this sponge-rubber barren, with clouds of mosquitoes cheering you on, was by no means a pleasant experience, even though one could always pause to investigate the little pitcher plants filled with water and trapped flies, and talk in guarded tones of the quicksand said to exist in some parts of the barren.

Strawberries and bakeapples were so limited in supply that they were used only for home consumption; blueberries were the real cash crop, for the forest fire of a few years before had ensured an unlimited supply, and when home needs had been filled, the surplus could be sold to the half-dozen market gardeners who went by once a week in their wagons. Because you could keep the fifty or sixty cents per gallon thus realized, all the resources of Eaton's mail-order catalogue opened up before you. Once, after poring wistfully over the steam engines, air guns, and erector sets, I was cajoled into the more practical purchase of an Ingersoll watch. In time this treasure arrived and worked beautifully for a whole week, after which no amount of persuasion could coax a tick from it and I was advised to return it for repairs.

With manly courage, I walked all the way to Port Morien and sent the watch to its destination by insured mail. But the Fates were most unkind; that night the post office burned down with my watch in it. Because I had the certificate, I expected to get my money back from the deal, but it turned out that by post-office regulations, jewellery was not supposed to be sent by insured mail, so my season's earnings of four dollars went up in smoke with the post office and did little to endear me to the Establishment.

On our summer calendar, Dominion Day, July 1, was relegated to its proper position of unimportance, a day in which, because the mines were idle, we all worked in the garden. Festive celebrations were reserved for the "Glorious Twelfth," the day on which 220 years before, King William had ridden in triumph over the base remnants of Catholicism. Previous to our acquiring the Model T, this was the day on which Father, Mother, and family usually made a brisk two-mile hike to Morien Station, caught the Express to Mira Gut, a thrilling six-mile ride, and, along with dozens of others, disembarked and headed for the steamboat.

For a six-year-old of that time a ride on the train was sheer ecstasy, but its memory soon faded in the light of what was to follow, a trip on a real steamboat up to Mira Ferry or Marion Bridge: clouds of smoke pouring forth from the stack, the gleaming bell, and whistle, and deck machinery, the nautical uniforms of Captain Phillips or Captain Nickel, the beautiful scene that unfolded as we chugged our way up-river. This was living.

On one of these memorable occasions I was the central figure in a dramatic story which constantly improved with retelling. It so happened that the family was promenading along a path high above the river, and as I strayed far in front of the group, my attention was caught by the antics of a boat wheeling in circles below. Suddenly my head met with a firm but yielding object which threw me flat on the ground. A slow Irish voice drawled indignantly, "You cawn see, cawn't you?"

It turned out that my head had met solidly with the protruding, carefully nourished abdomen of Father Brady, parish priest of Port

For a six-year-old a trip up the Mira River on the steamboat was more than sheer ecstasy.

Morien, who, prayer book before his eyes, had been moving on my orbit from the opposite direction. The horror I felt from this actual physical contact with a *priest*, a *real priest*, was to haunt me at night for weeks and resurrect all the tortures of the Spanish Inquisition. Father, on the other hand, was simply delighted by the incident, especially because it had occurred on the Glorious Twelfth. The glee with which he told and retold the story indicated that I had won a place in the pantheon of Protestant heroes, almost equivalent to that of King William.

One of the unfailing chores of a summer evening was going for the cows. After the morning milking, the local herd of seven or eight was turned loose with the option of going wherever they felt like going. Most of them were belled, and the tinkling could be heard quite a distance if the wind was right, but when you consider that they often travelled two miles from home in a day, and that this radius was largely a wilderness, finding them was by no means easy. Occasionally the search failed, and they remained at large all night, returning only in the middle of the next day to have their bulging udders relieved.

This search-and-find responsibility was shared alternately by the local youth. After due consultation with anyone who may have seen the cows during the day, you took off hopelessly in every direction, sometimes not arriving back home before dark. Sometimes one of the cows ventured out too far in the saltwater marsh at Deep Cove and became mired, or "stogged in the bog," as old man Mitchell would quaintly put it. Failure to rescue it before the tide rose meant certain drowning, so that was an emergency.

Fathers were duly notified and soon appeared on the scene with pries, ropes, and other pulling paraphernalia. Even if only the head of the unfortunate animal remained above the muck, somehow it had to be lifted and turned over on its side before it could be pulled to shore. Cries of "heave" and "now all together" rang out, and little by little the cow was pried out of the mud and hauled to safety. By this time the men involved in the operation could scarcely be distinguished from the cow, but strangely enough neither the cow nor its rescuers seemed to suffer any permanent ill effects, and the combined operation only served to unite the community in a feeling of neighbourliness by providing a topic of conversation.

One thing you learned from hunting cows was, each cow had her own personality just as a human being did. There were the old reliables, which, once started on the way home, could lead the others along, making correction unnecessary; others were of an erratic disposition and inclined to wander and engage in leadership disputes; some were just plain ornery and mean. Unconsciously, you were inclined to associate the cow with its owners, and this led to a more tolerant attitude toward animals.

It was part of our moral training that youthful hands should not be left idle, so before leaving each morning, Father left Mother a list of tasks for the children: potato bugs were to be gathered at one cent per dozen, the rows of potatoes were to be hoed, rows of vegetables were to be weeded, the barn to be cleaned, duff to be collected on the shore and stored in bags awaiting transportation, eel grass to be piled on the shore for collection. Only when the day's assignments had been completed were you free for play. Recreation usually took the form of swimming, and as for many years we did not own a boat, we had to depend upon the Esserys to take us out to the channel, or at high tide, down near the cemetery, where we peeled off our clothes and swam in the nude, unless objectionable girls were present. You learned to swim at an early age by being thrown into water over your head.

Some release from unpleasant chores might be granted if you were going trout fishing, for that could ease the food bill. Fishing brooks were numerous within a five-mile radius, and such activity could scarcely be regarded as work. Food-storage problems were much more acute in summer, the only refrigeration consisting of lowering the food down into the well in a bucket. Fresh meat appeared on the menu only after Alex MacLeod came up from Port Morien in his butcher wagon on Friday. Although he had ice in his wagon, the slow trip in the heat ensured a high aroma, but it was assumed that you had "summer complaint" anyway.

Christmas was, of course, the most exciting time of the year: the arrival of Santa Claus and his reindeer. Under the existing circumstances this belief seemed much more credible then than it possibly could now; the world was a small place, and miracles were constantly happening.

It was quite possible that he *could* get down a fireplace chimney, even if it were crooked; sometimes you saw claw marks in the chimney where he had knocked off the soot.

Before long, though, rumours began to circulate surreptitiously that the whole thing was a father-mother plot to improve conduct and morale. To disprove this cynical opinion, a week or so before one Christmas I began rooting around various hidden recesses in the house, and sure enough, there they were—Christmas presents, all carefully marked and labelled! To say that I was disillusioned is a vast understatement. Like Adam, I had eaten from the Tree of Knowledge and no longer could inhabit Eden. I sat disconsolate in the parlour for a long time trying to assess the implications of this unwished-for discovery.

In the end, pragmatism was to triumph; the presents appeared as usual and so did I. What did it matter? If parents found such sordid deceit amusing, it would be just as well to play along with them for a while. Otherwise the presents might not be forthcoming. By the time the Christmas goose had appeared on the table, things had settled down to normal.

Turkeys had not yet reached our bill of fare, but the goose was to prove of much greater utility; you not only ate it for dinner, but the quarts of grease derived from the cooking process was to provide the elixir of youth for the next three months. When you had sniffles, it was rubbed on your chest; if you had a cough, it was spooned down your throat. It was the universal specific for all ills up to March, then you needed a spring tonic. The first of these was a repulsive mixture of sulphur and molasses; the second, the vilest concoction of all, was prepared by boiling together the bark of cherry and dogwood (mountain ash) trees. The horrible bitterness of this infusion was certainly enough to guarantee its medicinal properties. It was *good* for you. As it probably contained some vitamin C, this may have been true, though our unfailing supply of native berries, over and above the orange you received in your stocking at Christmas, should have supplied this need.

Another mysterious medication, this time for the prevention of chronic nose bleeding, derived from Grandmother Murrant. If you suffered from this affliction, she bored a hole in a nutmeg, put a string through the hole, and tied it around your neck. The irrationality of such a charm becomes all the more annoying when I recall that at least on two occasions it worked, putting a permanent end to the nose bleeding experienced by my brother Harold and me.

In any direction from home, except eastward, we were surrounded by miles of unbroken, scrubby, second-growth spruce, fir, birch, and poplar, criss-crossed with occasional trickling, swampy streams, a natural habitat for rabbits and muskrats. It seems likely that rabbits had provided a good deal of the winter fare for our ancestors, for their skills in snaring them had been passed on to our fathers. When the leaves had fallen, but before the snow had arrived, these rabbits, which were later to change to winter white, still wore their brown coats, making them conspicuous objects to hunters who could easily bag a half-dozen in an afternoon. The regular food supply, however, came from snaring them, with techniques probably learned from the local Indians.

Early in the fall you could simply search out rabbit runs in the undergrowth and stick a loop of brass wire over them. In winter we were taught to construct long "hedges" of spruce or fir, interspersed with openings. In each opening a pair of stakes, "gateways," were driven into the ground about five inches apart and notched near the top. Between the notches was placed a cross-stick, the "toggle," to which the snare was attached and fitted between the gateways, while a cord from the toggle was attached to a "spring-pole," a convenient alder or spruce branch. Caught in the snare, the rabbit soon displaced the toggle from its notch and was whipped off the ground and garotted. Piles of young birch were placed on each side of the hedge to lure the rabbits through the gateways.

Tramping through the forest each morning to the snares was always an exciting adventure, and you could come home with seven or eight rabbits each day. The cruel and forbidding aspect of this was that at times a rabbit was snared around the mid-section rather than around the neck and was still alive and kicking. No one enjoyed bashing him over the head with a stick until his piteous screams had ceased, but it had to be done.

Prominent on the winter menu was fried rabbit, rabbit stew, and rabbit potpie. The latter was prepared in a large baking dish by Mother, covered with a thick pastry, and browned in the oven. It was a gourmet specialty, a welcome variant to the salt-cod, salt-herring and salt-pork diet. A quarter of beef did not go far in winter with a large family, and while there was always the homegrown pig, most of the pork ended up in the salt barrel, probably because the pig was killed before the frost. Regardless of the fare, however, at the Peach table you ate what was on the menu or suffered banishment; there was no nonsense of likes and dislikes. On a number of occasions I was chased from the table for refusing to eat salt herring (one of Father's delicacies, which I loathed) and secretly fed by Mother later on.

While the muskrat population did not rival that of the rabbits, many of the trickling, swampy brooks had their families. Trapping them, of course, was much more exciting than snaring rabbits, for they provided a quick cash income. Here we used steel traps with a carrot poised on a stick above the pan of the trap, and tried to ensure by means of a sliding cable that the muskrat could drag the trap into the brook and thus drown himself. Without such a device, the unfortunate creature would often chew off an entrapped paw and thus escape.

At home the catch was carefully skinned, the pelts drawn taut on a wooden form and exposed to dry in the kitchen, providing a rather musky odour. Shipped to Halifax or Montreal, pelts at that time could bring from three to five dollars each, a real windfall for the youthful trapper of the 1920s.

Looking back on this "nature period," I am comforted by the fact that rabbits and muskrats now flourish in their lairs untroubled by the human race and that beavers have returned to their ancient haunts in the area. Within the past ten years trout have been taken at the old bridge, indicating Nature's patient triumph over man's greedy and disgusting style of operation. If berries still abound, they are left to their original claimants, the birds.

Winds rustle the leaves on the quaking aspens that have completely engulfed the old wash plant. Where gleaming locomotives roared down the grade with their trains of coal, a high embankment stripped of rails pursues its mysterious course through the wilderness, whose silence is broken only by the cries of loons and the ringing evening notes of the hermit thrush.

Decades ago the glorious Mira River steamboat rotted away at its moorings and was towed to its final resting place in a junkyard. Its captains, too, have long departed to their great quiet. So perishes man and his works?

Fraternal Feuds

Chapter Eleven

In a family of six, with birthdays spread over a period of twenty-two years, it inevitably happens that the older members of the family have little association with the younger ones, for the former will have grown and left home before the latter arrive. This was the situation in our family, and I did not really get to know my younger brother and sister until we had grown to adulthood, and then only as a result of casual encounters. Also, in the nine years that elapsed between my birth and that of my brother Stewart, momentous social and family changes had occurred, so that to a great extent we grew up in separate worlds. By the time he was ready to enter school, my private world, as I recall, was already on the point of disappearing, and we had entered the modern age.

Over the years parents have a habit of mellowing as they find no great disasters have fallen upon them as a result of the decisions they made concerning their children, and that these creatures seem to thrive almost as well under a certain benign neglect, though, perhaps, only the more fortunate ones ever make this blissful discovery. Add to that that in later years the family financial position is usually more secure, and there is a good case for arguing that the older members of a spread-out family have a much more difficult time than the younger ones.

For five long years my brother Harold, as the only son, had occupied the centre of family attention and had become the monarch of all he surveyed, when to his utter bewilderment, all this was to change in the twinkling of an eye with my inopportune arrival. I have always felt that he could never quite forgive me for being born, nor his parents for having brought about such an unpropitious event. Only in this light can be explained the stresses and strains of our resulting future relationship. I was to be the victim of the only real sibling problem in the family.

Saying this does not imply, of course, that a state of constant hostility existed between us, for when it suited his purpose, he could be extremely

There was a nine-year age difference between Earle (right) and his brother Stewart. They grew up in separate worlds.

pleasant to me, and I found his attention flattering. I was soon to learn, though, that his ways were more devious than mine and that somehow or other I always wound up with the short end of the stick.

In most ways he was my complete opposite: where I tended toward plumpness, he was tall and thin; while I needed constant activity, physical or mental, he could spend unlimited time just sitting and staring into space. He engaged constantly in violent arguments over trifles with Father, while I soon learned to avoid disputes that could not possibly be won. In extra-familial relationships, even allowing for the age differential, he was more affable and relaxed than I, a fact which I probably envied and resented.

The most astonishing thing about this fraternal relationship is that it was never to change. When, as adults, we met on increasingly rare occasions, our greetings were warm and friendly, but as the evening wore on, over a few drinks, the banter we exchanged, good-naturedly at first, always seemed to degenerate into half-seriousness and one-upmanship, which showed that our basic feelings had not changed. The extreme shock I experienced at his sudden death, in his late fifties, was probably compounded by feelings of guilt and regret that now the last chance had disappeared of resolving the ancient problem, though in reality there was no solution.

Up to the age of fifteen or sixteen I was to endure his physical dominance, scorn, denigration, petty persecutions, and was outwitted at every turn. At that point, as a measure of self-defence, I embarked upon a physical-development program à la Charles Atlas and in a short time overcame the physical handicap of a five-year age gap, at which point that type of superiority ceased, but there were others.

It seems strange that upon the few occasions I was to witness his come-uppance, fate was to conspire in bringing it about without my conscious aid. The first such incident occurred when he was about seventeen and had begun to cultivate his personal appearance, to "dress up," whether the occasion demanded it or not. It was easy to tell that he felt quite handsome.

One bright Sunday morning he put on his best togs, even a handkerchief casually protruded from his breast pocket, and announced that we were to go rowing on the brook. Naturally, I was to do the rowing, while he, the Grand Seigneur, was to do the sitting. It turned out that the rowboat had been partially filled with rain overnight, so he stood on the rear thwart of the boat preparatory to bailing it out. After he had bailed for a minute or so, it seemed to me that I could speed the process by pulling the boat further up on shore, thus concentrating the water within his reach. This I did in all innocence (believe it or not), and hearing a wild cry, I turned around to see him flailing his arms, like a bird's wings, in a very fine balancing act. This was followed by a tremendous splash, and there he was swimming, hat still on his head, out in the middle of the stream. Well aware of his tendency not to accept apologies and regretful explanations, I took off for the tall timber and remained there the rest of the day.

In a second incident involving his self-abasement, I was to play only the role of a delighted observer. Because the Peach family was never to own a horse, Father had borrowed Old Perry, Uncle Ab's faithful steed, and sent us to haul home some bags of duff he had piled on the shore about a mile away. We duly harnessed Old Perry to the two-wheeled cart and set off on our adventure. Not long after arriving on the scene, we were stranded because one cart wheel had given out. There was no question as to how I would get back home: I would walk! Brother Harold, though, had other ideas. He was going to ride.

Now, Old Perry was one of the most gentle, complacent farm horses in Cape Breton (no one could accuse him of being spirited, as was Bess,

Uncle Tim's horse). His only problem was that he had never been ridden before. Unaware of this, my gallant brother detached him from the cart and, in the best Tom Mix tradition, went on to mount him and ride off into the sunset.

After a few analytical and thoughtful steps Perry came to the conclusion that he didn't like a weight on his back. In real rodeo style he first threw up his rear end, then his front end, completely sun-fishing his rider, who almost immediately came tumbling down onto the dirt. Then Old Perry galloped for home. I was astute enough to conceal my delight under the proper expression of concern as to my brother's welfare.

When I no longer feared Harold physically, our practical jokes on each other resolved themselves into a friendly feud and one-upmanship. He had arrived at that period in life where nocturnal rambling in quest of females often kept him out until one or two in the morning, at which time the rest of the family was sound asleep. Feeling a natural disappointment at how he was getting away with murder, I decided to make his quiet, discreet entrance less effective by stacking up against the kitchen door every pot, pan, and bucket in the house. When he entered at two o'clock, the resulting quake must have registered at least seven on the Richter scale and awoke the whole family, resulting in an orgy of mutual recrimination.

In the long run, though, quite unknown to himself, he was to rub salt into a wound that festered for years. Urbane, sophisticated, travelled, he had returned on a summer trip from employment in the United States, and one fine evening with rare generosity invited me to accompany him in a quest for girls, two of whom we picked up in short order.

A year or so before, unfortunately, I had expended upon the attractive, chubby one all the hopeless, unspoken, long-distance idolatry and devotion that only a pubescent teenager can summon up, even reaching the point of weighing her three-year seniority as an impediment to a future marriage. If she accidentally happened to smile upon me, I knew that in the end, true love could only triumph over such a minor obstacle.

While this attachment had moderated to some extent by the evening under consideration, I was scarcely prepared for what was to follow. After she had climbed into the front seat with Harold, my erstwhile love and my brother clung to each other and rejoiced as if they had known one another for years, leaving me to fend hopelessly with her unwanted and unattractive companion in the rear seat. To add injury to insult, we no sooner had reached home than he proceeded to regale me with his success in striking oil on the first try, a triumph which he continued to explore the remainder of the summer. I had made the introduction, and from that point he was to carry on alone.

Fortunately he was never to know of the bitter disillusionment he had inflicted upon me or he would have continued to twist the knife into the wound. In the face of his unwelcome revelations I maintained a stoic and inattentive silence, but I did not forgive or forget.

If history is any indication, fraternal relationships have always been difficult, and even murderous, particularly in dynastic families where a brother represented a rival to the succession. Cain's nasty precedent was at some time or other followed in every social organization that ever existed. Although such extreme measures were never taken within the families I knew, it is interesting to recall the relationship that existed among the Peach brothers of Port Morien, Father's first cousins.

All six were fishermen in the proper season and carpenters for the remainder of the year. All except Tom, the eldest, were small, dark, tough characters almost indistinguishable from each other, and it was said that their quarrels were fervent and unending. But if an outsider got into a battle with one, the ranks of the clan closed, and he had to fight the whole family, as Norman Ferguson, the gaunt county councillor was to discover. Having engaged in fisticuffs with Fred, he dragged his battered frame home after a combined operational assault by Murray, Hen, Ab, and Charlie, following which he was always to refer to them as "the dirty, little Peaches."

In contrast, relations among the governor's sons, if not cordial, were at least amicable and neighbourly, though minor disagreement did occasionally occur. As we had no horse, Father often exchanged his labour for the use of one of his brother's horses at ploughing time, the two brothers working together. On one of these occasions, when he and Uncle Ab were engaged in ploughing our front lot, an amusing and revelatory incident occurred. Old Perry had just reached the end of a furrow when a loud howl of anguish arose from the opposite side of the brook, where John Martell was accustomed to storing his fishing boat for the winter and refurbishing it in the spring.

"Sa-a-an-dy ... Sa-a-an-dy." The ploughmen paused to listen.

"Yes, Jack," Father shouted. "What's wrong?"

"Sa-a-an-dy," he sobbed, "they spilled all me paint ... an' I got nothin' left to paint me boat."

The ploughmen left Old Perry in the furrow and, accompanied by their two sons, walked across the bridge and over to the flat. John's face streamed with tears. Someone had not only spilled his paint but had also, between the stem and the stern on one side of the boat, written in two-foot-high letters "S-H-I-T T-U-B." It was the sort of prank that, had it happened to someone else, would have warmed the cockles of John's heart and caused him to guffaw endlessly. But this was different. He needed sympathy and, if possible, swift retribution.

Father gave me a grim, worried look. "Do you know anything about this, Earle?" Fortunately my innocence at this time would have disarmed a lie detector, and I was immediately exonerated. In times of great stress Uncle Ab had a strange habit of using his son's formal name when he addressed him. Ordinarily, he was known as Frank to all and sundry, but this was such a crisis.

"Franklin!" he said, gritting his teeth and his eyes narrowing to beady little points.

"Yes, Father."

"Franklin, did you spill John's paint?"

"No, Father."

"Franklin, are you sure?" Evidently, Frank seemed a little unsure.

"No, Father, I didn't." He shook his head and looked him straight in the eye.

"Do you know anybody that did, Franklin?"

"No, Father, I don't." Uncle Ab cogitated this denial for some time, shook his head, released a squirt of tobacco juice, and said grimly, "I dunno!"

As things turned out much later, his skepticism was well founded. Time was to reveal that Franklin had been at least an accessory *during the fact*. The mastermind had been Billy Murrant, Uncle Tim's adopted son, who had a positive genius for plotting acts of vandalism and getting away with them and, indeed, of not even being suspected of his crimes. As the only orphan of the community, he could draw on a good lot of sympathy and had cultivated the art of lying most convincingly to his foster mother, Aunt Annie, a distant relative. If she believed him, that was enough—and she always believed him. Later he was to care for her in her old age with the utmost devotion.

But for the moment John's tears were in vain. He had to buy more paint and repaint his boat, and no one could be *too* sorry, for his own juvenile streak sometimes led him into pranks that ill befitted an elderly man. One evening, as he was crossing the bridge preparatory to working at his boat, he spied Nell Mitchell, Amos's one-armed servant, sculling her way downstream in her rowboat. Nell was raw Newfoundland in speech and disposition and hence a natural butt for jokes. Running over to one side, John secured a big, flat rock and hid it on the bridge. When she came within range, he balanced his heavy burden and let it fall beside the boat, soaking her to the skin.

As the boat emerged from under the bridge, he scurried over to gloat over Nell's discomfiture. Unable to bash him over the head with an oar, she could only flay him with the sharpness of her tongue: "I tot yer dr'ars fell off."

Fundamentalist Puppy Love

Chapter Twelve

The previously noted migration, and subsequent conversion, to the Baptist faith of Anthony Martell's family was to have far-reaching consequences for us. Much of our early lives centred around the church which his descendants had built at Homeville and around the strict fundamentalist faith they had espoused. In its narrowest aspects this took the completely negative view summed up pretty well in the lines of the old hymn:

> This world's a wilderness of woe;
> This world is not my home.

Dancing, drinking, and card playing (with the Devil's cards) were taboo; even Sunday swimming was out, and only with special permission were we allowed to go rowing. In fact, every precaution was taken to ensure that on this one day in the week children would be denied all pleasures and left as miserable as possible. In the early years, then, we fidgeted around unhappily all morning, learned our Sunday-school lesson, had the main meal of the day at noon, and shortly thereafter set out on foot for Homeville for two-o'clock Sunday school. This was a dismal session indeed. Father usually taught the half-dozen members of the senior class, and if this included Adam Kelly, the heated arguments deriving therefrom, concerning the interpretation of certain passages of scripture, threw the other classes into confusion. Inevitably, at Sunday supper we would enjoy an extended summary of these theological subtleties to round off the delights of the day.

During a brief recess at the end of the lesson we wandered out into the yard, where the horses, with their attached wagons, were tethered to the fence around the cemetery, switching their tails madly to shoo off the mosquitoes which plagued man and beast alike. Then we went back

Life revolved around the church. On Sunday, dancing, drinking, card playing, and swimming were not allowed.

into the church for the main service. The itinerant and younger adults headed into the last two pews, where their propensity for carving on the back of the seats would be less obvious. But the recognized families all had a pew of their own; ours, fortunately, was adjacent to a window with a lovely view overlooking Homeville Lake, the beach, and, in the distance, Scatarie Island and the south side of Mira Bay. With this entrancing prospect before him as the preacher pronounced his text, mangled, twisted, and interpreted it, a small boy was far removed from the wilderness of woe and the moral lapses of ancient Hebrew potentates and prophets. He concentrated instead upon the deep blue sea and the patterns of the white clouds above it.

Because the congregation at Homeville was relatively limited, we shared a pastor with the Mira church, and the parsonage was located there. Even with this arrangement it was not easy to attract a full-time preacher, and often theological students of Acadia University served the parishes. During collection it was often the custom to have a singer or instrumentalist perform, and Father sometimes offered his tenor voice in the performance. The most memorable of the soloists, though, was Joe Phillips of Mira, the local Heifetz, whose soulful renditions of "Traumerei" and "Souvenir" plainly exceeded the cultural require- ments of his audience, who appreciated much more the excruciating grimaces which accompanied his performance. Beyond a doubt he was the greatest violinist in the area, but if he could have expressed upon his instrument the gamut of emotion that continually exercised his gaunt visage, he certainly would have ranked with Paganini.

In my more discerning years a permanent pastor, the Reverend W. Ferris, had been engaged to share the charge, a man with an extremely mechanical five-syllable laugh, "ha-ha-ha-ha-ha," which he employed on every possible occasion. The Reverend Mr. Ferris, though, was a devoted student of classical Greek, and many of his sermons involved quotations of the original Greek text with a learned commentary of all the possible English translations and interpretations which might be adduced therefrom. He was plainly happy in this intellectual legerdemain and quite unaware that it was completely lost upon a rural audience accustomed to hearing about the old, rugged cross. I know that Father, who was by no means a subtle man, often tried to get his point across, but to no avail. The Reverend Mr. Ferris was a completely unemotional man save for one enthusiasm—cars! In this, he was completely unbalanced.

Having started out with an old second-hand Model T, he somehow, year after year, managed to trade it in and appear on the scene with a bright, spanking new model. Eventually he owned a real status symbol, a McLaughlin Buick, indicating a source of revenue far beyond his means. But he was not really interested in status; he simply *loved* cars and could go on for days talking about them, taking us for drives in them, expatiating upon their excellences. Here, beyond a doubt, was the top car salesman in the Maritime provinces frittering away his time with Greek texts to most unappreciative audiences, a complete miscast! In later years, I believe, he did get into that field with a high degree of success, but he was then no longer a young man.

The Reverend Mr. Ferris was a pleasant man, but it soon became evident to the elders that the work of redemption could not be left in the hands of men such as him. When a fair number of boys and girls had reached their mid-teens, it was plain that a harvest was due and a new reaper overdue. Word was sent to headquarters for an evangelist, a preacher with a message right from the horse's mouth, no dallying around with Greek texts! They needed a man like Anthony Martell, and one always seemed available.

Although too young at the time to be numbered among the redeemed, I can recall at least two of these spellbinders. The first was the Reverend Mr. Phinney, a rather frail, extremely emotional young man with a sweet, high-pitched tenor voice. When he had exhausted the last scrap of agony from the crown of thorns and the nail-studded cross, he strode silently over to the organ and in a quavering voice embarked upon that tearful hymn "The Heart that Was Broken for Me." It was just too much; he broke down sobbing in the middle of it and had to pause to continue.

What rural adolescent could maintain composure before an assault of this kind? When the call came for those who wanted to be saved to walk down the aisle and shake his hand, not one tarried. Their sins had found them out, and the stage had been set.

It seems that such conversions in our locality depended not so much on the degree of sin rampant at the time as on the temperature of the water in Homeville Lake. This would have been uncomfortably chilly before the middle of July, so sin could reign triumphant up to then.

On an appropriate Sunday afternoon, people assembled from near and far to gather round the little cove in front of Uncle Will Holmes's house, the saved, the unsaved, the Anglicans, even some Roman Catholics, for the event had somewhat the same morbid fascination as a public execution. Then arose the strains of the question-and-answer hymn "Shall We Gather at the River?" When the chorus had reached "Yes, we'll gather at the river," the preacher took the first sinner by the arm and, cautiously treading out over the rough stones, reached sufficient depth to submerge him. Down he went, up he came, back to the shore, and out with another sinner, until each one had been completely immersed. It had to be done *completely,* no messing around with christening or holy water or Achilles' heels that didn't quite make it. It had to be done right!

On another occasion the Reverend Mr. W. was summoned, who, I believe, had a naval background, a man filled with lively enthusiasm, not quite so tear jerking as his predecessor, and having the good fortune of possessing a wife, a rather stout lady with a beautiful singing voice. When she had employed this instrument to raise emotion to the fitting level, he went after the sinners in a brisk, business-like style, smiling but in a "let's-get-this-business-over" manner equally effective in guiding them into the lake. It may be worth noting, too, that at a more secular level Mrs. W. could render on the organ or piano a most astounding performance of "The Robin's Return."

Such ceremonial occasions, of course, also provided an opportunity for our elders to get back on the beam. Having polished up their all-too-familiar prayers, they, too, joined the procession to the front to renew their commitments and were greatly rejoiced in the work. Attendance at Thursday night's prayer meeting rose sharply, family prayers on bended knees were resumed at home, and old animosities were laid aside for a term as they sang, "Blest be the tie that binds our hearts in Christian love," and later as they chorused,

> Shall we whose souls are lighted
> With wisdom from on high,
> To heathen souls benighted
> The Lamp of Life deny?

I am sure they did so in all sincerity, and on the next Sunday a few extra coins were inserted in the section of the offerings envelope for foreign missions.

My own trip to the water occurred in my early teens. It was not an event to be escaped in any way, for Father's hints about "joining the church" were becoming less subtle and casual. Although the occasion was accompanied by a high degree of emotion, it was not exactly the type aroused by the Phinneys and Ws; indeed, it was of much more earthy origin.

The truth was that I had become infatuated with a lovely cousin of my own age who did nothing to discourage my feelings. Her soft, young curves and yielding lips drove me into such a panic of adoration that I dreamed of her night and day. Our "affair" never developed beyond necking and kissing, for though I was well aware of the goal and aims of sex, I felt she was much too "pure" to be associated with such desires. Anyway, my sex education had been limited to the usual "dirty stories" and Father's progressive outlook in insisting that I accompany him when our cow was to be serviced, neither of which could be tied in with the adoration of the virgin.

A further cooling effect on sexual adventures had been provided by a blue-covered book called *The Light of Life*, hidden in the bottom of Father's trunk in my parents' bedroom. To put a hand on this holy of holies was a risky business; to extract a book from its bottom, to open it, and to gaze therein was to court damnation in this world and the next. Yet such is human curiosity that I am sure that each of my brothers and sisters had their turn with *The Light of Life*.

This nineteenth-century treasure had been written by a clergyman. Neither its illustrations nor its text was lust-provoking or calculated to make the sexual act attractive; it was a business which men had to perform and women to endure in order to end up with a family. Any deviations from the God-imposed duty, any attempt to escape from the inevitable results of this joint performance, could only end up in disease, afflictions, ultimate disability, and incipient madness.

Given this secret knowledge, it is not surprising that I displayed a high degree of reticence and caution in relating to my beautiful adored. It was common gossip, too, that if you "knocked up" a girl, you had to pay a fine of five hundred dollars! I could just imagine Father's reaction to the news that he owed five hundred dollars because of his wayward son's misbehaviour. The son would undoubtedly have been cast into outer darkness. In light of these baneful possibilities, I kept my hands where they belonged.

On the subject of baptism, my beloved's brother, a close friend of mine, suggested that it was about time we joined the church. Not only he but also his dear sister thought so, which cast a new light on the idea.

This was something we could experience together—and so it came to pass. Three or four other youngsters went along with us.

After some discussion it was decided that the Reverend Ferris could handle the matter to the satisfaction of all. It would be a question of arranging things not too enthusiastically—no sobbing, no extended confessions of sin or proclamations of a contrite heart. He was just to make an appeal for a show of hands on the part of those who wished to join the church.

At an appropriate time we made the agreed-upon gesture, and in due course, the water in the lake being at a balmy temperature, we assembled on the rocky shore of Uncle Will's cove. The Reverend Mr. Ferris had donned his long waders, and in full view of assembled believers and curiosity seekers, he led each candidate in turn into the water and duly immersed him. My rapture was complete on seeing my beloved being led to shore, her long, blond locks streaming down over her shoulders— Venus arising from the sea! By some strange covenant we were now completely united, and no cloud threatened the future.

Oh, pains and raptures of puppy love! In a year or two she had seen the utter impracticality of our relationship and was being courted by a respectable working man a few years her senior. As for me, my life was to be plagued with such adulations up to the age of twenty, when a respectable married woman in charge of a girl's camp took me by the hand, led me to her cot, and gave me a practical demonstration of "the light of life." In the aftermath of this continued affair a blatant and immature cynicism possessed me, and I never recaptured the first fine raptures of puberty. A damned good thing, too!

In retrospect, it is distressingly easy to be cynical with the old-time religion of Homeville Baptist Church, particularly when it engenders bigotry and intolerance and over-weening self-assurance, as it so often has done in the past. So many of its adherents, in their human frailty, soon presume to have a monopoly upon truth, and even today the members of a derivative sect can stand, pamphlets in hand, on street corners, looking with pitying condescension on passers-by, saying in their hearts, "I'm giving you the chance! If you don't take it, it's not my fault."

In our situation, however, religion and the church filled a vital need in the community, a social need. It not only gave meaning to the everyday vicissitudes of life, of which there were many, but also provided the only opportunity for people to get together, either on Sunday or at the Thursday prayer meeting. At least two generations of their ancestors were buried in the little cemetery behind the church, and they were still carrying on the tradition. Now they also lie with them, our fathers and mothers, the Martells, the Peaches, the Holmeses, some of the Murrants, and the Shepards. In 1970 the little abandoned church was torn down.

Year by year little spruces will thrust up among the graves and, as in so many rural Cape Breton cemeteries, will finally overwhelm the site and leave it completely forgotten. The same natural forces that changed Homeville Lake into a saltwater cove will return oblivion to those who briefly triumphed over them. *Requiescat in pace!* They were good people; not only good but also remarkable people in a literal sense, in that each of them, through his strengths, foibles, and peculiarities, had become so closely identified with our community.

Relatives, Neighbours, and Characters

Chapter Thirteen

Growing up as we did among the descendants of John Spencer, Arnold Holmes, and Charles Martell, we were, as far as I can remember, quite unaware of any special relationship to them, though undoubtedly our parents were aware. Children are interested only in what is at hand, and among these descendants were certainly some interesting and amusing characters. Two of the Spencer great-grandsons, Willie and Albert, still lived, as market gardeners, on part of the Spencer grant on South Head. (Willie's problem as a fervent, drinking Baptist will be noted later.) Albert, a tall, thin-moustached man with a tiny head perched dangerously on top of a long, spindly neck, always reminded me of Happy Hooligan, a comic-strip character of the time. Howard, a third great-grandson, married Father's sister Kate, raised a family, and came to a sad, suicidal end. Our most immediate Spencer neighbour was grandson Robert, popularly known as "Old Rob," of whom more anon.

Through infant mortality and failure to marry, the twenty male grandchildren born to Arnold Holmes's five sons had been reduced to three by 1925, and these left few descendants. This in contrast to the Spencers and Martells, who still proliferate there and have spread widely into the United States and other parts of Canada.

Uncle Tom Holmes was a pillar of the Baptist church and of the community. A slight, elderly, heavily moustached man, he lived partly by fishing but depended chiefly on a small vegetable garden on the western side of the lake, part of the original Holmes grant.

Once a week we met him in his horse and wagon en route to Glace Bay, a few burlap bags thrown over the meagre load behind the seat. Sometimes he stopped in Black Brook to pick up the blueberries we had picked during the week. A nasal defect of some kind caused him to snort violently at the end of each phrase, and this, combined with a simultaneous scratching of his crotch, identified him so unmistakably in our minds that even our most fledgling amateur actor could take over his role in our eel-spearing game, for Uncle Tom was the inveterate eel spearer of Homeville Lake, which was just outside his door.

I can still see him before me, a heavy, dark cap on his head, a full-length overcoat draped over his spare frame, prodding earnestly through a hole in the ice into the murky depths of the lake, where the eels had hibernated in the mud for the winter. He was a confirmed tobacco chewer, as were many of his peers, his brand being the soft, rich variety known as King George's Navy. If he spat, it was infrequently, for always when teaching Sunday school, he allowed the delicious juice to trail down his throat, the effluvia staining his graying moustache and running down his chin.

A man of the utmost probity, he could employ for his protection, when necessary, a certain native shrewdness, which was aided by the fact that he was notoriously hard of hearing and heard only what he wanted to hear. Uncle Tom knew instinctively all the best eeling spots in the lake but liked to reserve them, when possible, to himself. Thus when the spearing was good, he did not leave his catch writhing around on the ice as many did but paused to conceal them in a sack. When approached by another spearman, the following dialogue might ensue:

"Gettin' any eels?"

"Eh?" Hand to ear ... hand to crotch.

"Ya gettin' any eels?"

"Sorry. Can't hear ya." Motions repeated.

"Are ya gettin' any eels?" the other party shouted.

"No ... no eels. Scarce this year." Snort ... snort.

He and his wife, Anne, were poor and lived a minimal existence. As far as I know, he had no sons and only one daughter, who had married a Scottish neighbour and produced a large family, also as poor as church mice. In spite of this, the measure of respect Uncle Tom enjoyed in the community was evident when his house burned down with everything in it. The neighbours, one and all, joined together to build him a new one, which in a fashion, is still standing. It was done at no cost to him and was probably one of the last gasps of the pioneer spirit.

His brother "Uncle Will," whose property took in the north shore of the lake, was another community fixture. Another market gardener, he was fortunate in having produced sons and daughters who could contribute to his welfare in his old age. A stout John Bull type, he puffed and blew at the end of each sentence, thus stirring the sparse hairs of a white moustache. His reputation for piety was outstanding and probably deserved, for he missed no opportunity of public prayer in church. In fact, every youngster in the church could repeat his prayer word for word without even pausing and by employing the same creaking, high-low falsetto, which invariably ended with, "... and may we all have a free course and be glorified. We ask it in Thy name. Amen."

In spite of his goodly size, there was always something puttery and womanish about him, which may have increased his reputation for piety. Old Rob Spencer, the Rabelais of the community, used to relate a tale relevant to this: "Now, looka here ... I'll just tell ya about Will. Ya know me and Will was out cuttin' fence poles on Arnold Holmes's back lot. I was limbin' down a long spruce when me axe slipped an' took Will fair in the arse. Looka here, I thought the man would bleed to death. But d'ya know, so help me God, there was nothin' come out of him but pure buttermilk. Hor! Hor!"

His son Robert, about Father's age, had spent considerable time in the United States as an electrical engineer and, having amassed some money, returned to live with his parents and establish a large fox farm. This, in the days when black and silver foxes brought fantastic prices, must have proved a lucrative enterprise, and the Holmeses must have left quite an estate to distant heirs. "Will's Rob" was the victim of a severe speech defect, stammering so pitifully that he had difficulty in making himself understood, a handicap which naturally identified him to us in our eel-spearing game.

Near the church, on the highway to South Head, was the Homeville Post Office, administered by Adam Kelly, a stout, elderly, potbellied potentate of Irish extraction who claimed New Brunswick as his native land. Any product labelled with this point of origin was automatically proclaimed the best: "That's good turpentine! It comes from New Brunswick."

For his second wife, Adam chose Siddie Holmes, daughter of Galen, and inherited along with her not only part of the Holmes property but also her brother "little Rob," a dwarf whose four feet of height may have matched his intellectual stature. In spite of this, Adam's Caliban could do the work of a full-grown man, and he needed such an assistant, for he was fat and toddled around puffing.

Adam Kelly was Father's chief adversary in Sunday school, and their finger-pointing arguments and vociferous shouts often beguiled the tedium of these sessions. Essentially, though, Adam Kelly lived through the boredom of the year in anticipation of the "Glorious Twelfth." He had reached such eminence in the Orange Order that he was assigned the privilege of riding King William's white horse in the annual parade in Glace Bay—and this was status! It is understandable that Siddie was extremely proud of him as, bejewelled and besashed, he rode in the sunshine down Commercial Street amid the thundering band. This also made him a somewhat august figure in the community and certainly entitled him to disagree with Father, who, though also a fanatical

Orangeman, somehow failed to attain such a position of high degree.

Adam administered his duties at the post office with pomp and ceremony and shuffling of legal documents. It required at least a good half-hour to get a money order made out to Eaton's, and the learned effort and technique necessary to accomplish this subtle *tour de force* found him quite exhausted at the end of it. You felt that you were imposing upon his good nature by burdening him thus and that it would be better for all concerned to have the job done in Port Morien. It was true, too, that the Kelly residence was inevitably pervaded with the overpowering reek of mutton fat, as the elder unproductive members of the flock fell victim to a gargantuan appetite.

Midway on our daily travels to school, on the northern extreme of the Holmes grant, we passed the green, gabled house where Ronald Holmes (Rannie) and his sister Kate lived with their aged mother, Isabella. Ronnie had a huge 275-pound body, a red face set on a head that maintained a constant reedlike trembling, short-sighted eyes that darted in every direction, and an explosive, stammering speech that defied analysis. A hard-working farmer, he, too, depended on his vegetable garden and prospered, for his was the best land in the area.

Adjacent to the highway he also had an excellent apple orchard, fenced with barbed wire and guarded by a large German shepherd named Bruce. Such a formidable combination constituted a challenge to our native ingenuity. When the red astrakhans ripened, we often success- fully employed a ruse that involved sending some of the group to the back door to buy apples while others crept through the woods, climbed the fence at the rear, and went to work. Some of us had severe moral misgivings about such deceit, especially when the decoys reported on how nice Kate had been to them. Kate was a lady in the best Victorian tradition and gave music lessons to some of the children, but when presented thus, a challenge had to be faced.

Ronnie was an inveterate and constant pipe smoker. One day, while repairing the roof of his largest barn, which, incidentally, was filled with hay, he removed some boards preparatory to replacing them, puffing all the while on his pipe. Suddenly, to his consternation, the pipe slipped from his mouth and vanished down the gap into the hay. A long moment of tension! Would it catch? In a minute or two, alas, a thin wisp of smoke arose, and by the time he had scampered back to terra firma, the barn was a mass of seething flames.

"N-n-n-never again!" he swore. "N-n-n-never goin' to s-smoke again! T-t-t-oo bad! T-t-t-too bad! G-g-g-great loss!"

His new-found spirit of abnegation increased the vibrations of a trembling head toward the speed of light. A week later, though, when we met him in his wagon on a remote part of the road, the usual train of tobacco smoke was still ascending. When he saw us, he quickly stuffed his pipe into a pocket, for he was a man of integrity and self-respect.

One sunny winter day he was the startled victim of juvenile viciousness and malice. Cousin Frank and I were returning from a rabbit-hunting expedition, with our shotguns, when we saw Ronnie coming down the road standing on a sleigh bottom drawn by his faithful horse Old Dick. Old D-d-d-dick, we knew, was a skittish horse. It was just too good a chance to miss. We hid in the woods until he had drawn abreast, then the two guns roared out as one. Old Dick's first jump carried him at least fifty feet. Ronnie remained on the sleigh bottom, but not in a vertical position, as he and Dick moved rapidly from our view. It was fun, but not a feat to be proud of.

Midway between home and Ronnie's, at the bottom of a sharp grade where huge stones protruded onto the highway, a road turned off directly to the left and led to the domain of Robert Spencer (Old Rob). The original Spencers in the area had, as noted, been John (1775-1827) and his wife, Clorinda (1787-1866), but their grant was situated on the south side of the inner part of Morien Bay and included the present site of the little Anglican church. His sons, Henry (1826-1893) and Theopholis (1828-1912), received grants on the opposite side near Black Brook, and the latter's son Robert occupied this land, at the time under consideration, with his wife, Marion Huntington, and their family. The original home, nicely remodelled, is still occupied by his pleasant daughter Edith and her husband, Allison Ferguson, a cousin of mine.

The Spencer domicile is well situated, commanding an extensive view of the inner bay. To the east, a little peninsula known as the Point, extends into the shallow tidal flats, and not far away lies the channel into which Black Brook discharges. A mile to the east of this lie the two bars separating the inner and outer sections of the bay.

At that time the sand flats abounded in clams, which provided fare not only for the family tables but also for innumerable clam bakes, the social events of the younger generation. A thick growth of eel grass covered part of the flats, and this, storm-driven on neighbouring shores and gathered thence by rowboats, gave us our winter banking for the houses. As most of these were situated on loose stone foundations and in effect open underneath, banking was a long-time tradition, and I propelled many a weary boatload from Spencer's Point and Spencer's Island into the landing at Black Brook, a task often made more arduous by contrary winds.

The Spencers, though neighbours, were not quite part of the inner circle, for they were Anglicans. True, some of them, probably through marriage, had embraced the true faith, but this had not included the family of Theopholis; Robert enjoyed a drink, and his family played the

Devil's cards: clubs, spades, diamonds, and hearts. At home we could play the same games, but we had to use a playing deck known as Nations: Africa, America, Europe, and Asia. On one occasion Mother had confiscated from under my pillow, mercifully without informing Father, a secret deck of the forbidden cards. Comment was unnecessary.

A middle-sized, heavily boned man, Rob in his infancy or youth had suffered an accident which caused the left corner of his mouth to be drawn permanently in an upward grimace and to the left, and although this disfigurement was partially concealed by a heavy brown moustache, his speech always seemed to issue from that side of his mouth. His left eye drooped at the outer corner, and the tear duct on that side tended to dribble, especially when he laughed, which was frequently.

Beyond doubt this deformity must have had a debilitating effect upon his personality development, and his genial derogation of our ancestral idols may have been an attempt to show that he was at least as good as they. But it did not prevent him from acquiring a lovely Huntington wife and lady, and their relationship always seemed close and warm. It was significant that, when identifying any member of the family, he invariably prefaced the name with "our"; thus "our Nelse," "our Nettie," etc., which could only indicate that they had *two* parents instead of *one*, as some of the fathers of that time would have preferred to proclaim.

Rob lived chiefly by vegetable farming and, having three strong sons, had developed a remarkable division of labour in the planting of his crops: "Now, I'll just tell ya how we put out our cabbage plants. Now, first of all we make the rows, ya see? Then I send our Nelse along with the hoe to make holes about eighteen inches apart. Ya follow me? Then I send our Bobby along the row with a bucket of water, ya see, to put some water in the holes. Along behind our Bobby I send our George with a bucket of plants. He puts a plant in each hole, ya follow me? Now then, I come along behind with another hoe and pack in around the plants. Ya get it? Now, I'll just tell ya, looka here, it don't take no time at all to put out a whole bucketful of cabbage plants."

It is no exaggeration to say that Old Rob was the revealed subconscious of long Puritan generations. Sexual problems must have arisen from time to time among the Martells, the Holmeses, the Murrants, the Shepards, the Peaches, and the Spencers, for many of them produced large families, and somewhere along the line deviations from the norm simply had to occur. Everyone knew of them, even Grandmother Jane Peach, who in her rare mental aberrations was wont to chastise community delinquency, but people in full possession of their faculties did not talk about such things. Old Rob was an exception to the rule. His scandalous anecdotes of our illustrious ancestors could oversupply three Peyton Places. It was not that he did not *respect* them, but that he found a saturnine glee in the fact that they, too, had feet of clay and were just human beings.

His bawdy yarns covered the generations: he knew who had got whom into the woods at the box social at Horn's Road fifty years before, and could detail exactly what had happened; he knew the treatment that had been prescribed for old Lauchie "No-Pail" when he married a young girl and found he was impotent; he knew the sons and daughters that belonged outside of the families they were in and who the real fathers were.

He was at his best when a faraway gleam shone in his watering eye and a hoarse chuckle came from the twisted corner of his mouth that held the pipe: "D'j'ever hear old John Peach singin'? Now, looka here, Old John sits behind me in church, and by George, when they sing 'My Soul's Overcome by the Blood of the Lamb,' Old John comes right out with, 'my soul obertom by da breed of a ram'.

"D'I ever tell ya about old Joseph Holmes and his servant girl? Well, ya know Old Joseph's wife died, an' he was left in a kinda hard spot, so by George, he decided the smart thing to do was marry young Christy. Well, she didn't wanta go lookin' for another place, so she married him. Now, looka here, she only stayed with the old fella one night, an' the next morning she came over home in tears an' said, 'I'm not stayin' with that old man another night. Ya know, he's right full of all kinds of dirty tricks.'

"D'j' ever hear about the trick they played on old Ben Shepard? Ya see, Old Ben was crazy about molasses. He called it 'lasses,' an' every time he went across the bay to Cheap Jack's in Morien for his order, the last thing he asked for was, 'How about a little lick o' lasses before I go?' Now, looka here, some of the boys got on ta this an' thought they'd play a trick on him. Now, this day he rowed across in the boat with his wife and her sister Cindy. When he was leavin' Cheap Jack's, he said, 'How about a little lick o' lasses before I go. Hor ... hor....' They was ready for him and had the lasses all loaded up with jalap. D'jever hear about jalap? Ya don't see the stuff around any more. Now, I'm tellin' ya, if ya loaded a fella up with jalap an' aimed him, ya could knock a partridge off that clothesline over there. By George, looka here, he didn't get a hundred yards off shore when it hit him, an' the last they saw of Ben, two women was rowin' the boat and he had his arse stuck out over the stern. Hor ... hor."

Although not really members of the shining band, three more Homeville residents provided a certain comic relief from other-worldly matters. The first of these, old Neil MacAulay, lived with his wife, Sarah (whom he called Sarsar), at the eastern end of False Bay Beach, a rather desolate spot. At least one generation removed from the Scottish Isles, Neil had never quite succeeded in mastering the intricacies of the English language and relied mostly upon his native Gaelic. His location and his language problem thus restricted most of his *shared* conversation with his wife, Sarah, and it was rumoured that at home they engaged in loud, uproarious battles. This I am inclined to doubt—and for a very good reason.

Neil had long ago surrendered to Sarah at home and fought his gallant battles all alone. In his riding sleigh, covered with warm blankets, he traversed the icy surface of Homeville Lake. A fairly small man of rosy pink complexion, masked behind a huge, bushy white moustache, he could be seen gesticulating madly and heard shouting wildly a good half-mile away. These were interspersed occasionally with a gesture toward his riding whip and a minatory "ga-hait." He then resumed both sides of the violent altercation with remarkable dramatic skill and then continued on his way. No doubt Sarah was always the loser.

Near the other extreme of the beach lived the Tuttys, in ways other than marriage closely associated with the Covers of South Head. Old Joseph had sired a family of innumerable sons and daughters, all of whom were constantly engaged in legal battles with neighbours or with each other over fishing rights and land titles. Old Joe delighted in recalling the details of such manoeuvres, which often ended with, "So, Jim swore an' Eph swore an' Bill swore an' I swore ... and we all took our oats."

To do him justice, I have to admit that Old Joe had proper regard for the feelings of the tender sex. On a warm summer evening when the Peach family had driven its new Model T into his yard preparatory to buying a salmon, the breezes swarmed with flying ants. It was only normal that he should remark upon this infestation. Ordinarily, Joe bestowed upon these creatures the good old biblical name *pismires*, but seeing Mother in the car, he thought this rather profane, so he squeaked, "Da mires is out tonight, Ma'am."

A stone's throw from the Tutty residence stood the abode of Stephen Wadden and his wife, parents of the celebrated and irrepressible Ben, the bad man of Homeville and vicinity. Ben resembled nothing so much as the second villain in an old Wild West thriller. The wild, darting gleam of his eyes told of an impatience with worldly affairs which only violence could eradicate, and he sought this regularly in the flesh pots of Glace Bay, often returning scarred and battered, accompanied by his confederates Archie Peach and Matty MacIntosh in an ancient Model T.

In a memorable accident at Deep Cove involving this Model T, Ben could not really be held responsible, for he was asleep on top of the week's groceries in the back seat, and Matty was at the wheel. The real villain was Henry Ford, who had designed a car that required a driver with two good legs to drive it; Matty had only one.

And it was Ben who set out to summon assistance. After staggering painfully through the pitch darkness and rain for a good three-quarters of a mile, he reached haven at Charlie Dillon's (formerly Ronnie Holmes's) and reported tearfully, with many shakings of his head: "Bottom up, Cholly! Bottom up!"

May the kindred spirits in the Kingdom of Heaven be not too far removed from those of our lost community.

Dancing, Drinking, and Fighting

Chapter Fourteen

In addition to the church and the school, a third building played an important role in community life, particularly for the younger generation. On the South Head road, about one hundred yards from where it turns off from the main highway, stood Homeville Hall, a drab, shingled edifice whose origin in time is unknown to me, a sort of community catch-all. At various times it had served as a meeting place for such organizations as the Sons of Temperance, the Orange Order, the True Blues, and the IOGT, for miscellaneous remnants of regalia, banners, and staffs of these were stored in a dark closet at the rear behind the potbellied woodstove.

The box social, evidently a carry over from early pioneer days, had its own traditions of serving as a pairing agency among young, marriageable men and women. In preparation for it the girls (and their mothers) worked diligently in their kitchens on cakes, cookies, and other choice tidbits. A collection of those was then assembled in a square cardboard box decorated gaudily with coloured paper and ribbons to constitute a "lunch" for two people.

On the night of the social, each maiden brought her box and delivered it unmarked and unidentified to the auctioneer at the hall. At the close of the evening's festivities this individual assembled his treasures on a table on the platform and with gusto and subtle innuendo proceeded to auction off each to the highest bidder. If she already had a swain, he was expected to identify her work of art and, regardless of price, to outbid all competitors, thus entitling him to sit with her and eat the lunch. Unfortunately, though, if he displayed too great an interest in any one box too early in the game, his competitors could run him up to such an astronomical figure as five dollars. Machismo demanded such sacrifices for the beloved.

For unattached maidens the box was a hope chest, and they waited in agony of acute anticipation as the auction proceeded. Who could tell

Dances, box socials, and picnics were favourite pastimes.

what might emerge from the event, what romantic association might begin? After all, custom demanded that the boy who purchased a girl's box had the unalienable right of seeing her home when the affair was over. I suspect that many of our generation owe our parentage and existence to the box socials held in Homeville Hall in earlier times, and it is sobering to reflect that one's inherited genes may have depended upon the outcome of a public auction!

The chief recreation at such affairs had always been a pairing-off game called Tucker, which involved certain innocent convolutions around the floor to a musical accompaniment. But in the moral disintegration of the 1920s this Baptist concession to entertainment soon became too tame, and all too soon a box social could not be held without a dance, a *real dance*. To most of the elders, dancing was a sin, for as Father succinctly put it, "A dance is where the Devil gets his work in." Our limited home library featured a slim volume of confessions, very modest and unexciting ones, on the part of those who had been led astray by "split-tail devils" and betrayed through attending dances.

Despite such strong convictions on the part of the elders, the charms of the box social began to pale, to be replaced by dances usually organized by entrepreneurs from Port Morien. Of the "square" variety, accompanied by a fiddler, often Johnny Murrant of South Head, these were open to the public, and soon the foreign element from Port Morien and other centres of iniquity were frequenting them. Soon it was rumoured that drinking was taking place at the dances, and empty rum bottles were found out in the woods behind the hall—the Sons of Temperance hall! It was generally conceded, with much head shaking, that the "latter days" were at hand.

At the time of these calamitous developments my older sister was probably eighteen or nineteen years old and of a disposition to make light of parental injunctions; after all, other young people were going to dances. I can recall the first occasion of her stealthy eleven-o'clock return to the household. Father had stayed up beyond his usual hour, suspicious that his will had been frustrated.

"Where were you?" he inquired ominously.

"At the dance," she shrugged.

A long, pregnant pause followed as he tremblingly mustered his strength to put the vital question: "Did you dance?"

"Yes," she chirped, "yes, I danced." This was sheer bravado.

The resulting explosion rocked the household and woke every sleeping member. Father stopped short of doing her physical violence, but with difficulty. If she was going on with that sort of thing, she could get out. He wasn't having any of that in his family. If she was going around with split-tail devils, she could get out. There was the door! By this time Mother had appeared on the scene, attempting to pacify him, and when his fury had cooled a little, Sister slunk off to bed in tears. It was a terrifying occasion for all.

To give Father credit, though, he did have the vital ability to adjust to the inevitable and was likely assisted in this direction by the soothing advice of his wife. After all, it would be a scandal if he kicked out his oldest daughter. What would the neighbours say? In due course Sister's going to dances was tolerated, but not approved. She continued to endure periodic lectures on the evils of dancing but in the end went her own way and danced, and nothing happened. Nothing happened! No fire and brimstone fell on the Peach household, and as she aged, Sister became quite a conservative character, even a religious one. As a matter of fact her triumph over her father on this occasion gave her a taste for battle which both were to enjoy for many years, particularly in the philosophical field of fundamentalism versus evolution, in which there was never a winner.

The existence of a Sons of Temperance society in the past underlines the fact that the community was aware of the evils of strong drink, but despite Grandfather Tom's habitual morning tot of rum, not one of his five sons touched liquor to his lips, in contrast to their six Port Morien cousins, all of whom were moderate drinkers. This emphasizes the controlling maternal influence derived from the Anthony Martell migration from Mainadieu. Two of Grandmother's daughters, however, married problem drinkers. In the immediate neighbourhood John Martell enjoyed a drink, as did Rob Spencer. The Holmeses and

Shepards were teetotallers to a man. Father, oddly enough, felt that a brew made at home did not fall into the banned category and, upon one occasion at least, embarked upon a project to manufacture blueberry wine. He unintentionally reinforced its potency by putting it in a galvanized bucket to ferment, and even the new brilliancy of this container did not deter him from sampling his product, with almost disastrous results. He did become very ill, but anyone with less than a cast-iron constitution would certainly have died from metal poisoning. In later years if he could be convinced that the product of a bottle was really homemade, he would enjoy a drink and was not inclined to argue about the truth of such an assurance.

That an ambivalence could exist in regard to drink was perfectly illustrated in the personality of Willie Spencer, one of our market men and a pillar of the Homeville Baptist Church. No one, not even Uncle Willie Holmes, could pray more fervently at the drop of a hat than Willie Spencer. He gave generously of his limited means and unstintingly of his labour to forward the work of the church and was, withal, a pleasant man and a good neighbour. Yet on the return journey from his weekly market trip to Glace Bay in his horse and wagon, Willie was frequently under the benign influence of strong drink, and it was considered fortunate that his old horse knew its way home.

None of his peers, though, could find it in their hearts to condemn him for his transgression and could only murmur with heads shaking and deep feeling, "Poor Willie!" And poor Willie became the perfect example of how drink could lead a man to destruction, except for the fact that it never seemed to do him any permanent harm. He was ashamed of his derelictions and swore on every occasion that we would never repeat them, but he always did and suffered no great injury therefrom.

Despite the fact that Prohibition was in full force from the early 1920s onward, no difficulty seemed to exist in procuring supplies of liquor, particularly of rum, or of what passed for rum, the favourite beverage of all true Cape Bretoners. Part of this supply came from the sea and the remainder from the LIP (local initiative program). Why, on our way from Black Brook to the Homeville school we passed daily one of the largest distilleries in the county.

Originally one of the old Holmes properties, this house and farm, located a quarter-mile north of the Homeville crossroads, had for some time been occupied by a Jewish family named Fine, and one of the children, a boy, was in my earlier grade in school. Eventually the Fine family moved to Glace Bay and sold their two hundred acres, much of it bush, to a Russian named Holton (at least he was said to be a Russian). A rather pleasant, young-looking man, though he cooperated in the organization of the local telephone company, he minded his own affairs and expected his neighbours to emulate his example.

Ostensibly a farmer, Mr. Holton was accustomed to making his weekly trips to Glace Bay by wagon, his produce covered with the usual small tarpaulin. In a year or so, however, it became common knowledge that the RCMP was not only interested in his activities, but also had already confiscated a still hidden in the thick forest on the back of his farm. Strangely enough, the community's reaction to this development was one of amusement rather than of indignation and alarm. After all, he was a good neighbour and a pleasant fellow who wasn't hurting them in any way. In the course of time Mr. Holton and the RCMP played many such games of hide-and-seek. I can recall an occasion when he came to pay his telephone tolls. Father asked him, with a twinkle in his eye, "Did you get another still yet, Mr. Holton?" "Yes, Mis'r Peach," he replied, "an' I got it hid dis time where Gott 'imself couldn' fin' it." And for a while this was so.

Whether the Almighty did run across it and betray him to the RCMP is uncertain, but the Mounties got their man. Moonshining can only be accomplished by combustion of some fuel, and combustion produces smoke. This had proved his downfall in the past. His native ingenuity, he thought, could overcome this problem.

He undermined the large embankment on which his house stood, timbered it up carefully, and built his still in the excavation, connecting it to his basement so that the smoke could exit through the chimney on his house, all carefully concealed. By this time, however, the RCMP probably had his marketing operations under surveillance and came one day with no compunctions about tearing the place apart. With his underground activities thus revealed, Mr. Holton regretfully concluded that moonshining was no longer a viable proposition, sold his place, and left for parts unknown.

On at least two occasions, while Prohibition was still in vogue, Morien Bay was the scene of the "tight-little-island" scenario. Rumrunners from St. Pierre or the Barbados constantly lurked outside the three-mile limit of southeastern Cape Breton, where they made rendezvous with entrepreneurs from Glace Bay and Sydney. This is a storm-tossed area, especially in the early autumn, when the Caribbean ladies sweep up along the coast. In such *sauve-qui-peut* circumstances the bay seemed a welcome refuge from peril, which in an easterly gale it is not, and they ended up with their cargoes racked up on the rocks of South Head.

Such glad tidings swept around the area like wildfire, and soon every liquor-loving citizen within a radius of fifteen miles lined the bay coast of South Head waiting for the manna from Heaven to wash inshore through the breakers. Kegs of rum! Kegs of *good* rum, the real black stuff that scarcely changed colour when diluted with three parts of water and even in that condition could still burn its way to your toes!

It was not enough just to salvage a keg, or kegs, from the roaring sea; you then had to hide it or post a guard over it to protect it from hijackers, and because the RCMP had a noxious habit of being represented on such ceremonial occasions, it usually had to be hidden and rescued at a later date. In their frantic haste it was not always possible for the rescuers to take proper bearings on the place of concealment, and for weeks afterwards grim-faced seekers patrolled the coast, searching behind every bush and outcropping of granite for their precious load. I would be surprised indeed if some of these precious heirlooms are still not awaiting discovery, artfully concealed in the bracken, a tribute to the days when rum was rum.

Before autos came into common use, the only means of reaching Glace Bay on weekends was provided by the Sydney and Louisbourg Railway. Perhaps in recognition of the fact that the coal miners of Birch Grove and Port Morien needed an opportunity to blow off steam once a week, the company ran a Saturday-night special which visited these localities; it left Morien Junction at 7:00 p.m. and returned from Glace Bay at 11:00 p.m. Recognizing, too, that the clientele on these trips would be citizens bent on whooping it up, they thoughtfully ensured that the accommodations were distinctly third class: hard wooden seats bolted down to dirty wooden floors designed to absorb, successfully, the combined effluvia of chewing tobacco and rotgut alcohol.

Needless to say, in spite of the lack of amenities, the Special was always packed to the doors, and the late return trip offered all the excitement and thrills of three Irish barrooms erupting simultaneously, and in that tradition, fist fights were open; anyone at all could participate and display his badges of battle to his colleagues on Monday morning.

The older youth of Black Brook and vicinity often undertook these perilous pilgrimages, the "in" thing of the time, and on Sunday compared their experiences and related them to an envious younger generation who could hardly wait to grow up and participate in them. The thrill of eating liver and onions at a real Chinese restaurant, of seeing Tom Mix and Hoot Gibson at the Savoy or Russell theatres, of standing around on Senator's Corner and watching the fights or the girls, amply compensated for a two-mile walk to Morien Junction through the pitch-black darkness—the epitome of romance.

Of course one could sometimes see movies in Port Morien. Tom McInnis, a local one-armed entrepreneur, had rented the Orange Hall and on Saturday nights often ran competition with Glace Bay. The unfortunate aspect of this venture, though, was that Tom's projector was completely unpredictable and suffered numerous breakdowns during each performance, any one of which might spell *finis* for the evening. Loud and prolonged groans arose each time the machine rattled toward a halt, and all too often rose to a tumult as, after a half-hour wait, Tom appeared in front to announce to his audience: "Ladies and Gentlemen, I am very sorry to announce that we won't be able to continue the picture tonight. You can get back your fifteen cents at the box office, or you can keep your ticket till next Saturday."

One of the delightful aspects of the old silent films was the musical accompaniment, usually provided by a local pianist who attempted to suit the music to the film action. The unlimited skill displayed by these musicians is evident in an anecdote whose setting may have been Tom McInnis's theatre in Port Morien.

The feature for the evening was *Scenes from the Life of Christ,* and in the course of the film Christ was portrayed walking on the Sea of Galilee. The pianist paused for a moment in considerable perplexity, then a gleam of inspiration shone on his countenance, and he began to hammer out "A Life on the Ocean Wave."

The End of Childhood

Chapter Fifteen

How psychologically enervating and disastrous Miss MacKay's harsh rule was to prove to the tender sensibilities of her students I have no way of estimating. At that time, and for many, many years after, teachers were judged solely on the number of students successful in provincial examinations. If a teacher avoided strong drink, pregnancy, and got students through examinations, rare indeed would be any parental criticism of the means employed.

A much more tolerant attitude was usually shown to a school inspector, for it was recognized that his awesome role could scarcely be carried out without the proper use of a little stimulant. On Cape Breton, at least, it was conceded that if he did not involve second parties in accidents in the course of his trying itinerary, this was about all one could expect; back-country roads were usually appalling, and the burden of responsibility on the mind of such a man was beyond ordinary measure. It took a brilliant student to appreciate the keen perception such an inspector might display in his questioning of the class and the profundity of his inspired mind.

Miss MacKay, then, was a highly successful teacher. At age fifteen, and following hard upon my first bitter disillusionment in love, I received the coveted Grade Eleven Certificate with all the rights and privileges pertaining thereto. The year was 1925, a memorable one in the industrial history of Cape Breton, for early in that year the coal miners went on strike against BESCO (the British Empire Steel Corporation), a bitter and long, drawn out dispute over wages. The personal acrimony each miner felt toward this invisible empire can be judged by the recalled complaint of one miner: "B'ys, I don't mind Manager Simpson. I don't even mind Nicholson [general manager]. It's dat damn BISCO. If dey'd only get rid of him t'ings 'd soon be all right."

But everything was not all right; as the summer wore on and the coal shortage grew, bootleg pits appeared in abandoned pastures, and in the true spirit of free enterprise truckloads of illegal coal rumbled over the highways at night. Even though the "dirty" Mounties sneaked around and dynamited such sites of fruitful labour, they continued to proliferate. I can recall working at a few of these operations, some of them extremely sophisticated. Previous to the arrival of His Majesty's Armed Forces, roving gangs of miners from Glace Bay and vicinity started a campaign of store breaking. This was usually directed toward company stores, though attacks were expected nightly on privately owned stores in Port Morien and Birch Grove.

An arch-conservative, law-and-order man, Father never favoured strikes and strikers and disdained the bitter sarcasm of the vitriolic radical J.B. MacLachlan: "The guid old Cape Breton slogan: take it, it's better than nothin'." Family sympathy, of course, was directed by Father, and I should probably have long forgotten the whole affair except for a circumstance brought about by the coal shortage. At the old wash plant, a mile from home, lay thousands and thousands of tons of "duff," the washings from coal brought there thirty years earlier. Max and Sam Fried, two enterprising Jewish brothers from Glace Bay, seizing upon the heaven-sent opportunity to make a buck, put in a spur line from the Sydney and Louisbourg Railway and erected a trestle from which railway cars could be loaded. With a strike on, there was no shortage of labour at minimum wages, and here, along with Father, I earned my first financial rewards from hard labour, a hellish experience.

Under a blazing sun, enveloped in clouds of mosquitoes, men loaded the stuff into two-ton mining cars from seven in the morning to five in the afternoon for about fifty cents per car. Much finer than the duff that had washed down to the shores, this had been packed by years of rainfall into a consolidated muck; each shovelful, when pried up from the mass, weighed thirty pounds. As the trolley road was considerably higher than the working surface, an all-out effort was required to heave the load over the side of the car; a real chaingang operation at which, on good days, you earned two or three dollars.

Any flabbiness which a love of good food had bestowed on my frame soon melted away under this harsh regimen, and muscles, worn and torn in the first few days, soon hardened into iron. I was working with men and finding that I could do a man's work—a young man rejoicing in his strength. When Max and Sam, the portly Jewish brothers, came poking around to oversee their hired labour making money for them, I would not have exchanged roles with them for the world. I knew that if you put shovels in their hands and put them to work for themselves, both would drop dead within five minutes, and this was some consolation. Moses must have felt like this as he beheld the effete Egyptian overseers; now the roles were reversed.

Fortunately my period in the wilderness did not drag out for forty

In 1925, Cape Breton coal miners went on strike against BESCO. It was a long, bitter dispute, with troops being called in to maintain order.

years but only two months. By September the strike was over, and though the Frieds' operation carried on for some years, Father had returned to carpentry at No. 22 Colliery at Birch Grove, while I, quite unexpectedly, found I was going back to school, a business I thought I had finished with.

Up to that time Grade Twelve had been offered only in Glace Bay or Sydney, neither of which were within walking distance and hence out of the question for me. It so happened, though, that the manager of No. 22 Colliery had two children ready to enter Grade Twelve and, as the foremost citizen, no doubt succeeded in convincing the school board at Birch Grove of the advantages of having a local Grade Twelve. No sooner said than done. Nobody had ever thought of it before, not even in Port Morien, which had a much larger school population. It was a stroke of genius, the sort of thing you would expect from a man who earned at least three thousand dollars per year. As for me, after two months of grinding toil the prospect of returning to school had its charms.

The first two miles of my daily journey to Birch Grove School was through a wilderness traversed by a path worn down by the feet and bicycles of Black Brook residents who worked at the collieries. It passed the old wash plant, crossed the Sydney and Louisbourg Railway, and met a highway at No. 22 Colliery, from which point on, the area was settled. Since the mines closed in the 1930s, the first part of this trek has become an impenetrable jungle. Birch Grove today is a residential suburb of Glace Bay, and although its population has changed little in the interim, its neat homes offer a much more inviting prospect than those in its days of greatest prosperity. Regardless of what colour they were painted, all soon degenerated to black, except the school, which apparently had never been painted or much attended to and was merely weather-beaten like an old barn. It was a two-storey, four-room country school with an enlarged privy at the back. As far as I can remember, its academic reputation was correspondingly low.

But in the year 1925 a new era had apparently dawned for this establishment; Arthur Harris of Glace Bay, fresh from Acadia University with a B.A., had assumed the principalship and was to guide the destinies of grades Ten, Eleven, and Twelve for the next ten months and to be my first male teacher. The twelfth grade included my good friend and seatmate Layton and our mutual cousin Byron Ferguson of South Head. The two females of the group were a Simpson girl, daughter of the mine manager, and a sprightly, rather attractive Ethel Ferguson of Birch Grove, toward whom I was to transfer in some degree my thwarted affection for chubby Joyce.

Mr. Harris, a small, thin, bustling, pink-cheeked individual of the Boy Scout type, was a most pleasant and likeable personality, far removed from the virago who had directed my last two years. His weakness lay either in a lack of competent knowledge of the subjects at hand or a lack of confidence in improvising an answer to an impromptu question, for he invariably shielded himself by evading or postponing a direct reply by saying: "Well, yes. Now, that's right. We'll have to look into that. I'll take that up with you later." But "later" never arrived, doubtful problems remained unresolved, and you found yourself mucking along on your own. A well-organized, mature student like Layton could find a challenge under such circumstances and work out his own salvation. I am afraid that at the time I was neither, for my mind was on other things, and I had not yet learned to accept personal responsibility. I was not alone in this.

As opposed to Miss MacKay, Mr. Harris did not bother checking closely on home assignments or preparation, probably assuming a maturity on our part that few of us had yet attained. Consequently, most of my evenings were spent playing Auction Bridge, a new game my brother Harold had taught us while home on vacation. For this pursuit we spent the evening at Uncle Ab's for the Devil's cards were still *verboten* at home; cousin Roy Shepard thought nothing of walking six miles for a bridge game. Weekends were spent either in the woods with a gun, skating, or in an unsophisticated pursuit of female company, a new diversion—anything but schoolwork. The most boring text on our curriculum dealt with a mild case of philology, Bradley's *Making of English*. Of this, and from this, I learned exactly nothing. My limitations in French and Latin were equally memorable, to say nothing of mathematics. As the inevitable final examinations drew nigh, I did

Every day on his way to Birch Grove School, Earle Peach passed the old wash plant (in rear), where his father, Sanford (left), had worked before 1910.

indulge in some sporadic study, but did not begin with much confidence.

However, had we been aware of how examinations were to be supervised at Birch Grove and had the temerity to be dishonest, all, perhaps, could have been well; at least one student in the class had this advantage. The Supervisor of Examinations was "Big Norman" MacDonald, sometimes known as "Bigorman," a heavy-set local lush who swung a game leg in circles as he loped along with the assistance of a cane. Henry LaCointe's great establishment was only a quarter of a mile from the school.

Everybody, young and old, knew of Henry's. Although Prohibition's strictest mandates were still in effect at the time, somehow they never reached as far as Henry's, that elusive grocer whose displayed commodities were much more precious than the rotgut liquor concealed behind the counters. Somewhere Henry had found a secure source of low-grade alcohol and, with true Gaelic verve and enthusiasm, had learned to temper it with such chemical skill that from it emerged rum, scotch, rye, and what have you, all enclosed in innocent pop bottles. In a mining community such a man could only be considered a public benefactor, and this alone probably insured him against raids, though he must have had proper protection. Henry was a real nice, polite guy.

Bigorman, too, was a prominent citizen in Birch Grove society; everybody knew him and, if they did not approve, at least took care not to offend him, for he could be cantankerous. It was not his first term as chief of examination and would not be his last. He liked conversation and found the society of Henry's back room especially congenial. So having given out the papers for the period, Norman took off for Henry's and returned around the time they were to be collected.

Nor did he follow the example of most such supervisors, of seeing that all textbooks were removed from desks during examinations. They were there for easy reference and were extremely useful in that type of examination. Yet either basic honesty or fear of discovery prevented all but one member of the class from using them, and this person used them quite openly. In the denouement it paid off, for only Layton and the copier passed all the required subjects, but Layton had really known his work. Ironically enough, in light of developments much further off in the future, I received pass marks in all but the two English papers, which required a minimum of 50 percent. Anything over 30 percent represented a pass in other subjects, so my achievement in these was no great triumph; for the second time I had been weighed in the balance and found wanting. Parental reaction to this failure, as I recall it, was much more subdued than to the earlier one; in spite of some early promise, it was becoming apparent that I had no serious intention or desire to continue my education, and that was that!

Meanwhile, the situation at home had undergone drastic alterations in the last few years. After teaching in schools around the area for some time, my sister Nettie had immigrated to the United States; Harold had worked two or three years on the coal-mine bankhead and had left to join her at the onset of the strike, leaving me, the eldest of the family, at home. Grandmother Murrant had died in 1925 at the venerable age of eighty-eight, having outlived most of her contemporaries. In the same year my sister Jean was born, the last addition to the family, and my younger brother, Stewart, was six years old.

In retrospect, I can see this point as a watershed between two ages; up to this time nothing much had changed from what my parents and grandparents had known. In spite of juvenile, bitter-sweet feelings at the time, I know now that I loved the old times and secretly wished them to carry on. But the days of the pioneers had come to an end; the swish of motor cars across the iron bridge had replaced the clumping hooves of horses; humming telephone lines had ended the seclusion of scattered homes; instead of learning to entertain themselves, youngsters were sitting down in the evenings with radio headphones glued to their ears; the old fishermen-farmers were rapidly dying off; and a sharply increased cost of living was driving their descendants off the meagre, divided, and subdivided grants and into the towns or away to the United

States. The Land of Lost Content was merging into the Age of Discontent, and caught uncommitted between the two, I was still at sea. If I was to remain at home, I had only one prospect before me: a career in the coal mines. Thus in my sixteenth year I became an employee of BESCO at No. 22 Colliery and went underground as an ordinary labourer for the princely sum of $2.40 per day.

Coal Mining

Chapter Sixteen

Collieries 21 and 22 at Birch Grove had begun operations around 1910 on an extension of the Gowrie coal seam previously mined from Port Morien, four miles distant, a good many years before. Mining from there had extended southeasterly under Morien Bay as far as it was economically profitable, then in the opposite direction until a geological fault in the seam brought further progress to an end. Exploratory boring had indicated that the seam continued further on at a depth of thirty-five or forty feet, but as this point was already distant from the mine shaft, it had not been considered profitable and the mine had closed down. No record had apparently been kept of this knowledge, and one of these old test holes later provided my career at No. 22 with one of its more exciting events.

This coal seam, over five feet in thickness, sloped to the surface at an angle of about twenty degrees, and the mines there had been driven straight down the seam. Along one of its limits, known as the "upheave," it pitched up from the depth at an angle of sixty degrees. But where there was coal, it had to be mined, and the few miners working in this weird configuration had developed skills found today only in the taxi drivers in Funchal, Madeira. My own experience here was limited to clutching a twenty-foot length of two-inch pipe, dragging it and the accompanying tools upward from timber to timber, then to lose a grasp on it and see it whizz back to the bottom five hundred feet below. Downright discouraging!

In ages long gone there had been much exciting geological activity in the area, but all was now quiescent, and the only thought in the minds of miners and mine officials was "to get the coal out." The repeated question "How're you getting your coal out?" acquired the same general meaning as the nonsensical "How are you?", "How're ya doin'?", etc.

As I drove by the site of No. 22 Colliery in 1975, it was plain how thoroughly Nature can in a few years overcome the ravages of man; a

Earle Peach often stopped to watch the pit cars trailing up the bankhead of No. 22 Colliery.

scene of bustling activity and incredible noise had reverted to its quiet, pristine pastorality. Groves of aspen and birch almost concealed the few remaining slag heaps, and the trodden surface around the minehead had long been overgrown by masses of nodding wild flowers so characteristic of Cape Breton. Conservationists often seem to me too inclined to cry havoc about man's destructive capabilities, overlooking the fact that their strongest ally is the mere passage of time. But perhaps they are people in a hurry, while Nature is not.

In my last year of school I had walked past this spot daily, often pausing to watch the pit cars trailing up the bankhead, and giving absolutely no thought to ever working there. I often wonder now what I did give any thought to at that time beyond vague, erotic dreams of girls and a morbid, hypochondriac concern about my health. Aunt Lizzie, Father's youngest sister, had recently died of consumption (tuberculosis), and the knowledge that a blooming young woman in her late twenties could be dead within a year filled me with foreboding.

One morning on arising, I discovered that I was spitting blood! I kept this deep, dark secret to myself. When the prospect of being sent to work in the mine loomed before me, I knew that it was an automatic sentence of death. In spite of my rugged physique and apparent flowing health, I wouldn't last long there. How sorry they'd be when they found out what they had done. Just as well to be stoic about it, keep a stiff upper lip. How long this death threat continued I cannot remember, but I eventually discovered on my own that I was the victim of bleeding gums and staged a remarkable recovery.

Over the years this pattern has repeated itself many times with all the fatal and incurable afflictions known to man, until in my old age I have become cynical and distrustful of all symptoms and have learned to take the fatalistic view that until your number comes up, you're okay and I'm okay, but when it does, there's no way out. The alarming feature of this, though, is the thin margin of chance separating the two possibilities "to be or not to be." My years in the mine made it clear on many occasions that only a hair's breadth divides them.

Mother had filled another lunch can. At five-thirty in the morning I slung it over my shoulder and tramped with a few others over the familiar path along the washer drain, past the old wash plant, through the woods to Morrison Lake, and along the lake to No. 22 Colliery. In the wash house Newfoundlanders, Frenchmen, Poles, Hungarians, MacDonalds, MacRaes, and Smiths, bleary-eyed and sleepy, flailed a writhing mass of limbs in all directions as they wrestled on their pit clothes. Bearlike torsos, dirty backs (many miners washed only their faces), clean backs, bristly backs incredibly muscular, small retracted penises, huge flopping penises—obscene, good-natured kidding in a dozen dialects—these were the men who worked in the coal mine, and I was to become one of them.

I changed into my clean overalls and lined up with the rest at the lamp cabin, where, having presented a numbered brass disk, each received from the lampman the battery-powered headlight that was to illuminate his next eight or nine hours. At shift's end he passed his lamp back in the window for overnight recharging, and the lampman gave him back his disk. On that first day old familiar names seemed to reassert themselves, for the lampman on duty was Herb Spencer from Morien, and at No. 1 Landing I was detailed to a gang of four under the direction of Johnny Martell, an older son of our neighbour John Martell. My associates were Fred Peach, an elder of the Port Morien Peaches, and Melvin Brand, commonly known as Mulvy, a slight, puzzling, one-eyed youth in his twenties. We tramped down the "travelling road" to No. 3 and entered the main pumphouse with its glaring lights and high-pitched, whining motors. This part of the mine had been worked out years before and was now miles from the nearest coal face. Water from the inner workings was pumped out to No. 3 Deep, which acted as the main sump, and from there electric turbines propelled it up a four-hundred-foot borehole to the surface. We were to lay a new suction line from the pumphouse down to the main sump, about eight hundred feet away. I soon found out that this was to be no picnic.

Each section of the eight-inch cast-iron pipe was ten feet long and weighed eight hundred pounds and was bolted, through heavy flanges, to the next with wrapped and tarred joints in between. Using the proper technique, a strong man could lift one end of such a pipe, but only to show off. But weight alone was not the problem. Each pipe had to be transported on two "dollies," by man strength and pries, to where it was going, over the most fiendish obstacle course one could imagine. Abandoned workings in a coal mine soon deteriorate into a reasonable facsimile of Dante's *Inferno*; timbers rot out, allowing heavy falls of stone from the roof to block the water course. The entire roof seems to be hanging by a thread. Over a three foot gap between the falls and the roof, through cold, acidic pools of water, each of these damned pipes had to be dragged into place and buckled on to the line. As it lengthened, production fell off until we were reduced to one pipe per day. Water dripped silently from the roof; you had to work to keep from shivering. It was a good introduction to the evils of manual labour.

To give him his due, Foreman Johnny was quite a remarkable chap; both he and Fred were actually fishermen by trade and mine workers in the off-season. Good-natured and completely unflappable in the face of difficulties, he hummed or sang *sotto voce* the same old song day in and day out:

> Oh I wish I had someone to love me ...
> Somebody to call me their own.

He gave the general impression that one should not be in a hurry. There would always be work left for tomorrow. Fred, on the other hand, was a typical representative of what County Councillor Norman Ferguson neatly termed "the dirty little Peaches." A small, brown, wiry man hard as nails, Fred never stopped complaining in a whining, indignant voice. In his world nothing ever went right. "My Jesus, Johnny," he would say, "we didn't get much done today, did we? Christ, we'll all be fired if we don't do better than that." And his leathered, Popeye-like features contracted in spasms of pain. After an excellent lobster season, if you asked Fred how he had done, his reply would be: "My Jesus, we didn't do anything. I don't know how in the name of God we're goin' to live." To give him his due, Fred did have problems; he had married Johnny's sister, who had produced a brood beyond ordinary reckoning, and this was not surprising, for both were descended from prolific families.

A most redeeming characteristic of the human race is its adaptability to any circumstance and its rapid acceptance of the most unfamiliar and outlandish conditions as being the norm. When a week or so had passed, it no longer seemed strange to walk down out of the brilliant sunlight, out of the fresh air, into total darkness that took five or ten minutes before one's eyes adjusted to the reduced light of one's headlamp and one's nose accepted the fetid, mouldy air of decay common to a mine. Air from a huge compressor on the surface was driven down a carefully constructed air course, circulated slowly through all the work areas, and returned up the main haulage way, ensuring that no significant accumulation of deadly gases could occur. Yet in most places you were unaware of any air change. When you were working, sweat streamed from your body, but when you sat down for five minutes, you were shivering. Add to this the fact that you could seldom stand up without stooping except where the "roof" had been "brushed"; the coal seam was five feet thick, but in the air course, the chief haulage areas, an extra foot of shale was taken down chiefly to ensure that it would not fall down and block traffic or slow air circulation. This left a roof of solid stone generally considered safe. As coal seams went, the Gowrie seam was of generous thickness; the harbour seam on which Glace Bay collieries nos. 11 and 24 operated was only three and a half feet thick and required a great deal more stooping.

In a month or so the suction line was completed between the pumphouse and the sump, and a new turbine went into operation. Up to this point I still had not seen any coal being mined, but only where it had been mined. On my next assignment, as a pipefitter's assistant, I was, to use a Newfoundland phrase, to "get into de t'ick of it." At that time all coal-cutting and boring machines were run by compressed air, and as mining operations went forward, additional lengths of two-inch wrought-iron pipe, twenty-two feet long, had to be added to the existing lines in all double-shifted working areas, at the rate of two pipes per week. Our working tools were twenty-four-inch Stilson wrenches, our accessories a backload of couplings, nipples, elbows, and T-fittings and of course unlimited supplies of pipe which often had to be carried hundreds of feet to their destination. These probably did not weigh much more than a hundred pounds and, with a man on each end, could be carried with relative ease.

My new boss was Horace MacDonald, an individual whose make-up, even upon reflection, I would not attempt to unravel, except perhaps to speculate that through chance or drink or pure inertia, he had failed to find a role worthy of his qualifications. In his late thirties, Horace was of an oxlike, stocky build and had enormous strength. He was also a rather handsome guy reputed to be a famous Casanova. Maybe the women had done him in. With little formal education, he seemed to have a wide background in reading and yet tended to scorn anything he had derived from it as a lot of bunk. Because he knew I had completed high school, I was always contemptuously referred to as Webster. Pleasant and rather urbane at one minute, he could fly into the most violent and destructive rage at the spur of the moment, at which times it was wise to keep out of his reach. Fred Peach used to say of him, "That crazy bastard Horace will kill someone yet." In spite of this Horace and I got along reasonably well and ended up with a sort of sneaking admiration for each other. One just had to take pains not to annoy him.

To explain how coal mining used to take place fifty years ago, one must first explain how coal seams occur. Formed from the decay of vegetation in the Carboniferous Period of geological history, seams vary from a few inches to many feet in thickness, but any given seam is usually of uniform thickness, and covers a very large or very small area and, in its sloping, varies widely in vertical depth from the surface of the earth. If close enough to the surface, it can be removed by strip mining, removing the overburden and recovering the coal, a practice common in the United States which leaves a wasteland in its wake. A number of seams may overlap in the same area.

Where drilling has revealed coal at a depth of more than a few hundred feet, vertical shafts are driven down to the seam, and the coal, when mined, is transported to the bottom of the shaft and raised up in huge buckets. All mines on the Phalen seam around the Glace Bay area use this means of production. But regardless of where it occurs, coal is not easily recovered; packed into the seam as tight as the stone which surrounds it, it has to be ground, chopped, and blasted loose with dynamite before it emerges into daylight in the form with which we used to be so familiar. In either a shaft or slope operation, coal is recovered simply by driving tunnels through it, but not at random. The direction of tunnelling is in the hands of the mining engineers who know where they are going and what they are required to do.

At No. 22 Colliery the coal seam emerged to the surface, and as noted previously, the main slope had been driven down the seam. At one-thousand-foot intervals, landings or levels were broken off east and west from the slope; the term "level" is a relative one, for convenient operation preferred a slight slope in the level. At similar intervals along the level, "headways" were driven up and "deeps" driven down the slope of the sea, each conforming to the twenty degree angle. This might be more easily visualized by picturing a level as a road built horizontally across the mid-slope of a mountain; roads going up the mountain from it are headways, those leading down from it are deeps. At one-hundred-foot intervals up the headways and down the deeps, "rooms" were broken off, assigned numbers, and turned over to a pair of miners known at that time as "butties"; these did the actual mining. The average headway or deep could employ thirty pairs of miners paid by the ton for the coal they mined. A miner at the "face" could earn fifteen to twenty-five dollars per day, which in 1926 was a lot of money, considerably more than the mine manager earned. Within their room a pair of miners were the lords of creation, and God help anyone or anything that prevented them from "getting their coal out." This was free enterprise, indeed.

A few days ago a mining-engineer friend of mine remarked how miners had changed working under the present "longwall" system of mining, a much more productive arrangement employing specialists of one kind and another but lacking that individual incentive to "get the coal out"—no spirit of competition.

By the time I arrived in No. 22 Colliery, the first level had been completely worked out, as had No. 2 Level West. All operations were thus confined to No. 2 East. Miners still continued to moan about how good things had been in No. 2 West; according to them, the good times were all over. The nearest working area to the mine entrance was No. 9 Deep at a distance of one and a half miles, the furthest No. 16 Headway and Deep, a mile further on. Time later revealed this to be the limit.

Powered by a huge electric haulage engine on the surface, an endless steel cable, two inches in diameter and five miles in length, passed around a "bullwheel" at the extreme end of the mine. This served to bring down the empty one-ton coal cars (boxes) and take up the full ones. These were attached to the "rope" at convenient intervals by a "grab," a metal bar, one end of which hooked on to the box by a trailer-hitch device, while the other end, with viselike jaws, clamped on to the always-moving cable. The system moved at a constant speed of about two miles an hour and a high degree of agility and skill was required of "landing tenders," who "put on" and "took off" the full and empty boxes by tightening or loosening the jaws of the grab with a spindle. In an emergency the rope could be stopped by short-circuiting two bell wires strung along the main haulage way, thus signalling to the engineer on the surface, but it was a serious misdemeanour to do so unnecessarily. This double-track railway system had to be kept in continuous operation at all costs, but problems often arose, for at one point the steel cable went around a ninety-degree curve and had to be held to the middle of the tracks by a series of turning "jugs" attached to the roadway. If the rope came off at No. 2 curve, it meant a two-hour job to get it back on, tying up the whole mine. Along the straightway the rope was supported on rollers which had to be carefully greased, as did the jugs on the curve. The functionary who in my time performed this vital task proved to be one of the most delightful, if pathetic, characters in the mine.

Mining Men

Chapter Seventeen

Who his antecedents were no one seemed to know, but Freddie Taylor lived alone in a "little black shack" a half-mile from the mine. A short, pear-shaped individual in his mid-forties with a rather pleasant face, Freddie was not given to undue conversation with fellow workers; but then he did not need such solace, for he lived in a world entirely his own. Perhaps the solitary nature of his task contributed to this world of fantasy, for all day, grease bucket and swab in hand, he tramped the two and a half miles of black haulage way and seldom met anyone. So Freddie talked to the jugs and rollers and lovingly bestowed on each of them a distinctive, feminine name.

"Susan, you little bastard," he would complain petulantly, "what are you squealin' about? I guess you want some sap on your nose, eh?" And Susan got some sap on her nose. "Alice, you're gettin' kinda run down. Guess we'll have to get another girl instead o' you." "Look, Hazel, I fixed you up only yesterday. You got no business squeakin' like that now, have ya?" And so it went on.

Freddie's dramatic improvisations were so well known that it was common practice to conceal one's lamp and sneak up stealthily on him, as you might on a rare bird, when he was beginning his lunch. As he opened his lunch can, a typical conversation might ensue: "I wonder what they put in me can today." He opens it and gloats in an astonished tone, "Holy Jesus, a nut bar!" Needless to say, Freddie always packed his own lunch.

Once off the main haulage way all roads were single-tracked, which meant that a spare road, or "drift," had to be installed at each landing and at each room, one for the empties, one for the fulls. From each landing a "chain runner" took his trips of empties up the headway or down the deep by means of a steel cable powered by a "donkey," an air-driven hoisting engine.

For a good many years the mine ran on double shifts, with a complete turnover of personnel at 3:00 p.m. Dayshift began at 7:00 a.m., and by that time the miners were in their rooms. Typically, when a pair of men entered in the morning, they found the face of the room had been undercut by their counterparts on the nightshift. With an air drill (jackhammer) they bored two six-foot holes above the cut, inserted three or four sticks of dynamite into each, plus electric blasting caps, and sat back to wait for the shot-firer. In addition to his headlamp, this official carried a safety lamp to test for noxious gases. After hooking his one-hundred-foot cable to the caps, he sheltered himself behind a coal pillar, gave a twist to his hand generator and—BOOM!—down came the coal, fifteen or twenty tons of it, not shattered into dust but into fragments suitable for loading with a shovel.

The pair then pushed in their first empty from the drift and began to load. How long it would take them to "clean up" depended upon the supply of empties available. As each box was filled, they pushed it out to the drift and brought in another, attached their "tally number" to it for identification and continued loading. Six boxes filled the drift, at which point they had to wait for the chain runner to take the full trip away and bring an empty one. On a good day, loading could be completed by noon. Then came the task of setting the room up for the nightshift.

Timbers were driven into place to hold up the roof where the coal had been removed. Placed at six-foot intervals, these formed a straight line on each side of the road. Forward progress of the room was kept on centre by lining it up with two wooden plugs placed in the roof by surveyors. A fifty-foot pillar separated them from the adjacent rooms, and at intervals "cross-cuts" were driven through this to maintain air circulation.

The radial coal cutter was then wheeled in on a trolley, its post solidly jammed between the roof and the pavement, the machine attached to the bottom of the post, hooked up to the compressed-air line, and swung around like a machine gun as the picks of the plunger chopped away at the face of the coal. When finished, the thirty-foot coal face had been under-mined to a depth of six feet, but it was a slow operation carried on with an ear-shattering din and clouds of coal dust. Not a warm job, either, for the exhaust on the machine soon became coated with frost from the release of compressed air. This task completed, the men were through for the day.

Contract miners were an exclusive group; one had to be of a certain age and "taken in" as a butty by an experienced miner in order to "get at the coal." Often a father might take in his son, who, in the course of time, would take an oral examination and acquire his "mining papers," enabling him to be a fully qualified miner who could work with others.

Eventually all the rooms on a headway or deep were driven forward about five hundred feet, at which point they met the rooms driven from the adjacent headway or deep. This did not mean that all the coal had been removed, for pillars of coal fifty feet thick, intersected by cross-cuts, still remained between the rooms. The machines then began to chew into the pillars. When one had been partially removed, the thousands of tons of weight assumed by the remainder was sufficient to start the "crushing" process, and the coal began to disintegrate without cutting or blasting, a stage more dangerous than ordinary mining. As pillars were removed, all weight was gradually assumed by the wooden timbers. Water began to ooze from them as they cut into their cap pieces. Loud thumps resounded through the open spaces as they were further compressed. In mining parlance, "she was beginning to work." Finally, with an ear-shattering roar followed by a massive airwave, the whole roof collapsed into the empty space. She had "come in from the blueberries." Operations were finished in that sector.

It is unlikely that this type of mining exists any longer in North America. Now huge electrically powered monsters grind into the coal face and load the coal onto moving belts, which eventually loads it into the cars. As the coal is thus removed, the stone and overburden collapses into the empty space. The day of the old-time coal miner has vanished into memory, but when we contrast his lot with that of the miner preceding the machine age, it seems in retrospect to have been an easy one. Before the age of the cutting machine, coal was undercut by men lying on their sides and chopping away at it with handpicks.

What of the hazards of coal mining. In spite of its reputation of being extremely dangerous, I would say that with certain exceptions, it should not be more so than other occupations involving the use of machinery, providing that the rules are obeyed. Certain risks cannot be foreseen; one of these is the occurrence of "pots" in the roof. These are perfectly moulded cylinders of solid granite formed in the stone overlying the coal seam, weighing anywhere from two hundred pounds to tons. If they can be seen, timbers are placed under them for support; some, with a thin layer of coal around them, are not likely to fall. Others may fall at any time or may never fall. In my three-year period in the mine two men were crushed by falling pots.

At the bottom of one headway a "bunk" had been closed in, where a dozen of us often sat around to gossip and eat lunch. When we came down one morning, a pot weighing several tons had crashed down in its centre. Our escape from death had been a mere matter of timing; its existence had not even been suspected. A standard joke among the initiated concerned one of the higher-ups in the coal company, who, on learning that men were being killed by falling pots, demanded indignantly, "I think it's about time we found out who is responsible for hanging these pots around where they can fall on people."

The chief peril to coal miners comes, of course, from the accumulation of the noxious gases methane (firedamp) and carbon dioxide (black damp), the first being responsible for most violent explosions, the second for the sudden dropping off of victims without much warning. Normal precautions against their menace consists of maintaining continual ventilation through all parts of the mine, the prohibition of smoking and carrying matches, and the use of safety lamps by mine officials to detect the presence of gas. In dry mines, explosions have often been caused by the detonation of coal dust, a condition offset by proper stone dusting. This was not a problem at the Birch Grove mines, where water dripped from the roof in many areas. It would seem also that proper methods of ventilation must have been followed, for in all their years of operation no explosions occurred, though occasionally miners had been known to keel over in pockets of black damp.

Most miners were victims of the tobacco habit, and because smoking was forbidden under pain of instant dismissal, practically everyone chewed tobacco, the two main varieties being MacDonald's Twist and King George's Navy. A few pit ponies in the mine also cultivated the habit, to the point where they would nuzzle miners' pockets looking for a chew. My own memories of this addiction have to do with an occasion when, having finished our task on the lonely nightshift, two of us lay down for a snooze in the course of which I swallowed a large wad of the stuff. It did not improve digestion.

Safety lamps, carried in hand by all mine officials, were of special advantage to workmen like myself on day pay. These tiny points of light signalled the approach of major or minor mine officials, and measures were immediately taken to display a determined enthusiasm for the task in hand. Loafing on the job was a prerogative for shiftmen, and because these twinkling warnings could be seen from a quarter-mile off, only a fool need be caught sitting on his ass.

The coal-mining regime of the late 1920s was still a strict, authoritative society little challenged in daily operations by the Miner's Union; you did what you were told to do without argument. Younger overmen were inclined to be more lenient and relaxed in relations with their underlings, but the old boys belonged to the spit-and-polish school and stood no fooling around. One of these was Old Man MacIntosh. Probably in his fifties at the time, a small, spare, ascetic-looking, moustached individual, he had spent his life in coal mines and could be imagined in no other setting. Nor could one be truly recognized as belonging to the mining fraternity until he had received at least one dressing-down from this awesome figure. When in a rage, his invective beyond all compare, he closed his eyes, tilted his head toward Heaven, and broke into what was probably a well-rehearsed prayer for protection from the inborn stupidity and asininity of the human race.

My first exposure to this curling blast took place one day when we had left the job early and had headed up the air course to escape detection. When within a half-mile of the surface a red light appeared, coming our way, there was no escape. It was MacIntosh. Poking his safety lamp into our faces to identify us, he began rather quietly as if merely curious, "Holy Christ Almighty, b'y, where d'ye think you're goin'?"

"Well ... ah, you see we were kinda tied up for pipe, and we were going up to see about that shipment that didn't come down."

"Oh ... I see. You were tied up, eh?" He closed his eyes, tilted his head sideways and upward. "Holy jumpin' Christ Almighty," came the quivering roar, "there's no need for anybody bein' tied up in this goddam place. There are hundreds of leaks in the lines you could be tightenin' up. Get to bloody blue hell back where you came from and get to work."

For some reason the antecedents of D.A. McGrath, MacIntosh's opposite number on the nightshift, were more widely known—or rumoured. First of all, it was generally conceded that he knew more about coal mining than any other official in the company's employ; he had his manager's papers and had held positions much higher in the mining hierarchy than his present one of overman; extremely intelligent, of a speculative, philosophical turn of mind, he could discourse with conviction, authority, and penetrating wit on any topic you could think of. But as with many mining men, he had squandered these fine assets on alcohol and had drunk his way down from being a top dog, and only held his present position as a sympathetic offering.

It was commonly rumoured, too, that all his misfortunes were caused by a nagging wife, a real virago who, from time to time while in a rage, he was accustomed to pursue out of the house and down the street. But this alibi probably contained a bit of male chauvinism, for like the chicken-egg controversy, the alcoholic-nagging-wife syndrome has no definitive starting point and is simply action-reaction.

A small, dark individual like his colleague MacIntosh, D.A. was generally pleasant and well liked by the miners, whom he delighted to engage in long drawn-out conversations, until any crisis arose, major or minor, when he went completely berserk and foamed at the mouth. His red light, his cane, and his timebook, all symbols of his office, flew wildly in different directions. He threw off his cap and jumped on it, all the while letting loose a string of unbridled, repetitious profanity. When, in a short time, the fit had passed, he became abject and humble, inquiring in a soft, trembling voice, "I say, did anybody see my book? I say, did anybody see my cane? I say, did anybody see my cap?"

There was something pitiful and tragic about D.A.'s career, and the men generally felt a great deal of sympathy for him. Not so his hard-bitten colleague MacIntosh, who, after observing one of his volcanic rages, reprimanded him severely, "I tell ye right to yer face, b'y, ye're a goddam fool." Unlike D.A.'s explosions, those of MacIntosh were always well controlled and rehearsed, though still convincing.

Only on rare occasions were you likely to run across Jennings, the underground manager, a burly, round-shouldered character whose beady, myopic eyes peered at you from under bushy eyebrows, and *Mister* Haley, general manager, an awesome figure indeed, considering that he stretched upward to a height of five feet, had a tiny, calm, clean-shaven face, a quiet, high-pitched voice, and would have seemed much more convincing managing a bank than a coal mine. He was reputed to enjoy a salary of four thousand dollars per year, which rated him far above ordinary mortals and made him immune to the bitter, cynical remarks directed toward most authority figures. Why, Mr. Haley could fire anybody, even Jennings, just by snapping his fingers and was thus worthy of respect.

An End and a Beginning

Chapter Eighteen

Often, after a two-mile tramp through snowbanks in bitter zero weather, the prospect of getting underground seemed most delightful; here, day and night, summer and winter, were one. But when June rolled around and sunny weather returned, each day spent in the black, smelly depths seemed a day lost from life. A position had opened up on the bankhead, and summoning up enough gall to speak to the unapproachable Mr. Haley, I succeeded in getting it, even though it meant going on the nightshift from three to eleven, which in turn meant slogging two miles back home, often alone, in pitch darkness, and arriving home at one o'clock in the morning. On the bankhead I became one of a crew of six or eight on the picking belt and was to learn what eventually happened to the coal I had seen mined underground.

As the full boxes, attached at intervals to the haulage rope, arrived at the top of the bankhead, a man assigned to "taking off" removed the grabs, and each box ran singly into the "tipple," a rotating cage, in which it turned a complete revolution, upsetting the coal on the shaker screens. Holes of various sizes in the screens separated the coal into grades, removing much of the dust which became "slack," while the remainder fell on a wide, moving belt which conveyed it into the railway cars under the bankhead. Stationed on both sides of the belt, the "pickers" snatched out the pieces of slate and stone mixed in with the coal, thus cleaning it for shipment.

Eight hours of this, spent amid the incredible noise and vibrations of the coal shakers, was not exactly a picnic. Only by shouting into your colleagues' ears could you communicate with them, while the appalling black dust clogged your breathing apparatus. For this, I had left the solid comfort of the underground, where, usually, if you wanted to loaf for a while, you just loafed and nobody saw you. Here you were tied in with a bunch of old, uninteresting men who had done nothing for years but snatch pieces of slate off the belt and who gave you dirty looks if you missed any. After a few months of this, I got a transfer to operating the tipple, which proved slightly more interesting, though it involved nothing more complicated than pulling a lever at the proper moment. Here, it soon became clear, I had got caught up in a production line where my movements were being ordered by machines. Any slackening of attention could bring on a minor disaster, the responsibility for which could be clearly pinpointed. Amid all the tumult and shouting, my mind had a tendency to wander off in many directions; neither mentally nor physically had I been designed to become a cog in a machine. With the approach of winter, I was lucky enough to get a transfer back to my old job, as an underground pipe fitter, and there I remained.

My boss this time was Michael M., a twenty-five-year-old relative of a mine official and an unusual character indeed to find in a coal mine. Of average height and slim, straight build, Mike had been raised a puritanical Roman Catholic, evidently under the academic guidance of Irish nuns or brothers whose lilting accents still lingered in his speech. Mike crossed himself with reverence a dozen times a day, never cussed, never smoked, never drank, never talked about women. Like the tobacco chewers, he did a fantastic amount of spitting, but unlike their streams of brown expectoration, his spittle was pure, white, and abundant. Because this habit was unassociated with any catarrhal or bronchial condition, I can only conclude that Mike was actually getting rid of his guilt, for he plainly had such a hang-up about sex that he would walk a quarter-mile out of sight to have a really private pee instead of turning around and spraying the nearest timber. He never showered in the wash house, and took the delicate precautions of a mid-Victorian spinster in changing his clothes.

This paragon of purity, though, was not an unpleasant chap to work with if you could avoid topics involving any slighting of religion; a misstep in this direction and his face reddened, his lips tightened, and you saw Savonarola shining through in unmistakable light. To work was to pray, so he was a conscientious worker, took life seriously, and was working his way through various categories of mining qualification with a view to attaining his manager's papers. How well he succeeded I shall never know. He had a child's sense of humour, and his amusing anecdotes were those of a mild Sunday-school teacher; even then I was of a more Rabelaisian turn of mind, yet my strict Protestant upbringing left me uneasy in the presence of such evident fanaticism in the opposite category.

When the miners had driven slightly east of No. 16 Landing, the days of No. 22 Colliery were numbered, for they encountered solid stone; the apparent end of the seam. Later events revealed that it did not actually *end* there but had been faulted at some time in the geological past, that the rest of it lay thirty-five feet above, and this higher level had been

In the fall of 1929 Sanford Peach informed his son Earle that he would be attending Acadia University, in Wolfville, Nova Scotia.

worked out seventy or eighty years previously from the old mine at Port Morien. In my pipe-fitting role I became directly involved in this discovery.

One day, when a pair of miners in No. 16 Deep shot down their coal face, a highly pressurized fountain of stinking water poured down from the roof and filled up the workings so fast that they had to take to their heels, abandoning their equipment. That afternoon we were ordered to get down to 16 Deep to lay water and air lines to operate pumps. On arrival we discovered that water had backed up five hundred feet from the coal face and was still rising. Its horribly acidic smell indicated that it was coming from old, abandoned workings; they had broken through into something not connected with No. 22 Colliery.

Needless to say, it was not a happy time to be in No.16 Deep or in No. 22 Colliery, for if it was a major breakthrough the whole mine might be flooded. Little by little, though, confronted with a network of pumps, the grim tide began to slack off. At the end of a week the deep was emptied back to the coal face to reveal water pouring out from a borehole in the roof. Men braved the odorous shower to insert a three-inch wooden plug into the hole, supported it with a timber, and the leak was stopped.

The deduction from this event was that when the old Port Morien miners had reached their western limit, they had drilled a borehole in search of the seam, had found it, but had decided to go no further. Mining records at that time were fragmentary, and there was nothing to warn the operators of No. 22 Colliery that such a borehole existed; the nose alone, though, was enough to assure one that this sulphurous flood had been "cooled a long time in the deep-delved earth." It meant, too, that when stray pillars had been taken out, the days of this colliery had come to an end.

I had been in and out of the mine for three years and was now nineteen years old. That fall Father, in his infinite wisdom, revealed that the money I had earned over paying my keep would be used to send me to Acadia University. Like Dickens's Pip, I was suddenly confronted with great expectations. In a month or two I would be laid off at the mine, and the only alternative was possible employment in another mine at Glace Bay, ten miles distant. I'd had enough of mines; it was time for a change.

How long my parents had been planning for this I have no way of knowing; their hope that I would become a Baptist clergyman and emulate the example of the illustrious Anthony Martell may have been as old as my childhood interest in comparing bibles. I suppose that at this point if I had been sufficiently hypocritical, I could have gone along with this, and financially it would have been greatly to my advantage, for theologues at Acadia received free tuition and other benefits. But I had absolutely no inclination for such a career, and to enter it under false pretenses seemed repulsive to me. Later I was to meet a few so-called theologues who did not have to wrestle with such a finicky conscience, but I could never number them among my friends.

At any rate the Land of Lost Content, which even in the last five or six years had changed very perceptibly, was rapidly receding into memory. After I left home in 1929, I never spent more than a month or two at a time in the environment I had grown up in. Perhaps only in contrasting it with the complexities and aimless uncertainties of the 1980s have I reached the point of enshrining it with a halo. Perhaps the human tendency to do this is universal. But at one time I seem to have lived in a very happy and secure world.

Appendix

to Chapters Two, Three, and Four

*Direct ancestors of Earle Peach

Family of Charles Martell (1733-1819) and Ann Smith (Schmidt) (1739-1804)

Thomas (b. 1760)
Charles (b. 1763) m. Susannah Mehitable Wilcox
John (1767-1836)
Jane (b. 1770)
Anne (b. 1772)
Joseph (b. 1775) m. Patience Phipps
Elizabeth (b. 1777) m. Joseph Dillon
May (b. 1780)
Anthony* (b. 1782) m. Lucinda Holmes*

Family of Anthony Martell and Lucinda Holmes

Joseph (b. 1804) m. (1) Susannah Spencer, (2) Mary Spencer
Annie (b. 1806) m. Benjamin Spencer
Ruth (b. 1808) m. John Huntington
John (b. 1810) m. Lydia Spencer
Sophia (b. 1812) m. Samuel Spencer
Arnold* (b. 1814) m. Jane Lisby Huntington*
Charles (b. 1816) m. Adeline Patience Holmes
Anthony (b. 1818) m. (1) Eleanor Stout, (2) Kate McNeil,
   (3) Hannah Baker
Lucinda (b. 1820) m. Arnold Holmes (b. 1822)
Thomas* (b. 1823) m. Mehitable Susan Martell*
Caroline (b. 1824) m. William Lawrence Holmes
Jane (b. 1826) m. Wentworth William Peters

Family of Stetson Holmes (b. 1753)
and Anna Shurtleff (Cape Breton Branch)

Clorinda m. John Spencer (b. 1803)
Lucinda* m. Anthony Martell* (b. 1803)
Viza m. Joel Noel Shepard (b. 1806)
Arnold (1793-1866) m. Ann Martell (b. 1816)

Family of Arnold Holmes (b. 1793)
and Ann Martell

Elizabeth (1816-1818)
Galen Stetson (1818-1824)
Joseph Martell (1820-1868) m. (1) Ann Severance, (2) Isabella
    MacAulay
Arnold (1822-1874) m. Lucinda Martell
William Lawrence (1824-1893) m. Caroline Martell
Adeline Patience (1826-1922) m. Charles Martell
Galen (1829-1867) m. Sophia Ann Spencer
Anna (1831-1837)
Stetson (1837-1882) m. Annie MacAulay
Marie Jane (b. 1837)
Charles (1839-1846)
Anna Elizabeth (b. 1843)

Family of Robert Peach
and Jane Andrews

Martha (b. 1798)
Robert (b. 1804) m. Hannah Forbes
Jane (b. 1807)
Susan (b. 1808)
James* (1812) m. Margaret —*
Nancy (b. 1813) m. — Boutilier
Louise (b. 1814)
Thomas (b. 1815) m. Sarah Wilcox

Family of James Peach (b. 1812)
and Margaret —

John (1833-1924) m. Susan Andrews
Elizabeth Jane m. George Martell
Sarah Margaret (b. 1842)
Dinah (b. 1844) m. — Tutty
Mary Ann (b. 1846) m. Arnold Holmes (b. 1848)
Thomas* (1847-1908) m. Jane Levinia Martell

Family of Thomas Murrant (b. 1787)
and Orelia Payne Peters

Thomas* (b. 1813) m. Anne Boutilier*
William (b. 1814) m. Sarah Campbell
Hannah m. William Severance
John m. Margaret Howie
Louisa m. Joseph Dillon
Anthony m. Mary Campbell

Family of Thomas Murrant (1813-1888)
and Anne Boutilier

Louisa Jane (b. 1835) m. William Munro
William Henry* (1837-1907) m. Adelaide Martell*
Susan Elizabeth (twin of William Henry)
John David (1841-1911) m. Jemima Ann Dillon
Orelia (b. 1843)
Rachel Sara m. Charles Peters (b. 1871)
Joseph (1854-1935) m. Ann Wadden
Ann Elizabeth (b. 1856)

Family of John Spencer (b. 1746) and Esther Bunnell

Hezekiah (b. 1772) m. Fannie Rice
Matilda (b. 1774)
John (b. 1775) m. Clorinda Holmes
Nathaniel (b. 1777) m. Laura Payne
Betsy (b. 1779)

Family of John Spencer (b. 1775) and Clorinda Holmes

George (b. 1804) m. Mary Martell
Anna (b. 1806) m. Edward Dillon
John (b. 1807)
Clorinda (b. 1809)
Arnold (1810-1811)
Arnold Holmes (b. 1812) m. Sarah MacAulay
Hezekiah (1812-1825)
Nathaniel (twin of Hezekiah, d. 1813)
Elizabeth (b. 1815)
Mary (b. 1817)
Esther (b. 1819) m. William Huntington
Nathaniel (1821-1825)
Emily (1823-1825)
Henry Galen (1825-1893) m. Lucinda Martell
Theophilus (b. 1828) m. Anne Jane Peters